# This book belongs to

...Finn

My name is finn

Draw a picture of yourself

**MEGADOODLE** is exactly what it says – a book of doodling! **COLOUR**, **DESIGN**, and **DRAW** all over the pages and learn as you create. Find out about rabbits, robots, reefs, and lots more! Are you ready for oodles of doodling fun? Then turn the page and begin!

Help me **FIND** my way home through the muddling maze

**DISCOVER** why animals live underground

**DESIGN** an out-of-this-world movie set

HELP THE RABBIT **FIND ITS WAY** HOME THROUGH THE MUDDLING **MAZE**

**Moles** are one of the best diggers in the animal kingdom. Their big spade-shaped feet make burrowing a swift job.

DRAW MORE UNDERGROUND ANIMALS

Many people claim to have spotted UFOs (unidentified flying objects) in the sky, but none have ever been proved to be true.

DRAW YOUR OWN SET

# DOODLEPEDIA

Doodlepedia

## Now you see me, now you don't!
You could be surrounded by animals in a forest and not even know it.
Many creatures have evolved superb **camouflage** to help them hide.
Some look like a **tree trunk**, a **stick**, or a **rock**. **Chameleons** are masters
of camouflage and can even change their skin colour!

A chameleon changes colour depending
on its **body temperature** and
**emotions**. The warmer or angrier it
becomes, the brighter its colour.

# Who are you looking at?

You are able to check your **reflection** in the mirror because light bounces off the glass and into your eyes, which send signals to the brain. If a surface is rough the light **scatters** in different directions, but if the surface is **smooth** and **flat**, the light bounces off at the same angle as it enters, creating a reflection.

**Light** is the fastest thing in the universe. It travels at about 1 billion kph (670 million mph). It's so fast, it could travel around the world **seven times** in one second!

The **primary colours** of light are red, blue, and green. **Combinations** of these colours make all the other colours, including white.

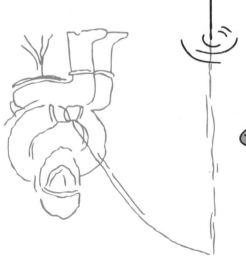

**DRAW** THE REFLECTION OF EVERYTHING ON THE RIVERBANK

# DRAW YOUR OWN TV SHOWS

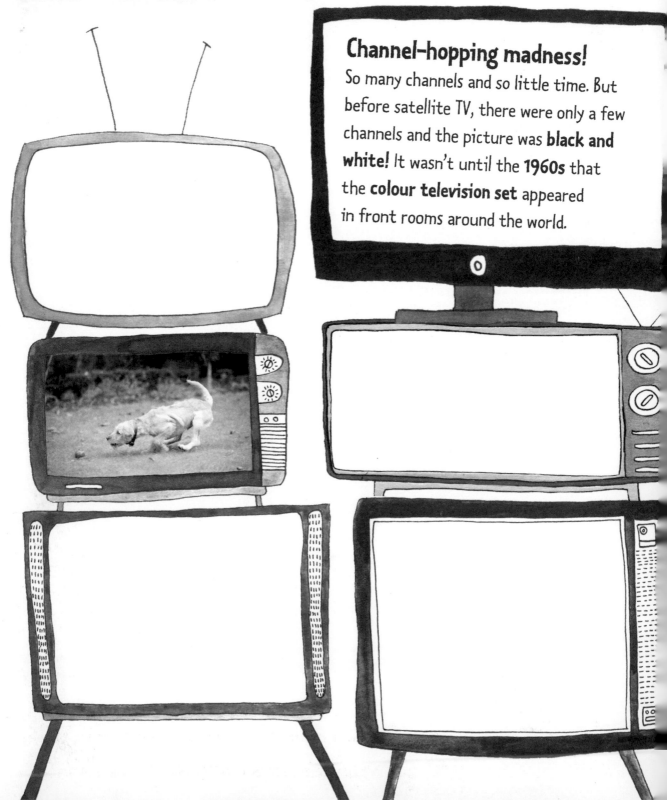

## Channel-hopping madness!

So many channels and so little time. But before satellite TV, there were only a few channels and the picture was **black and white!** It wasn't until the **1960s** that the **colour television set** appeared in front rooms around the world.

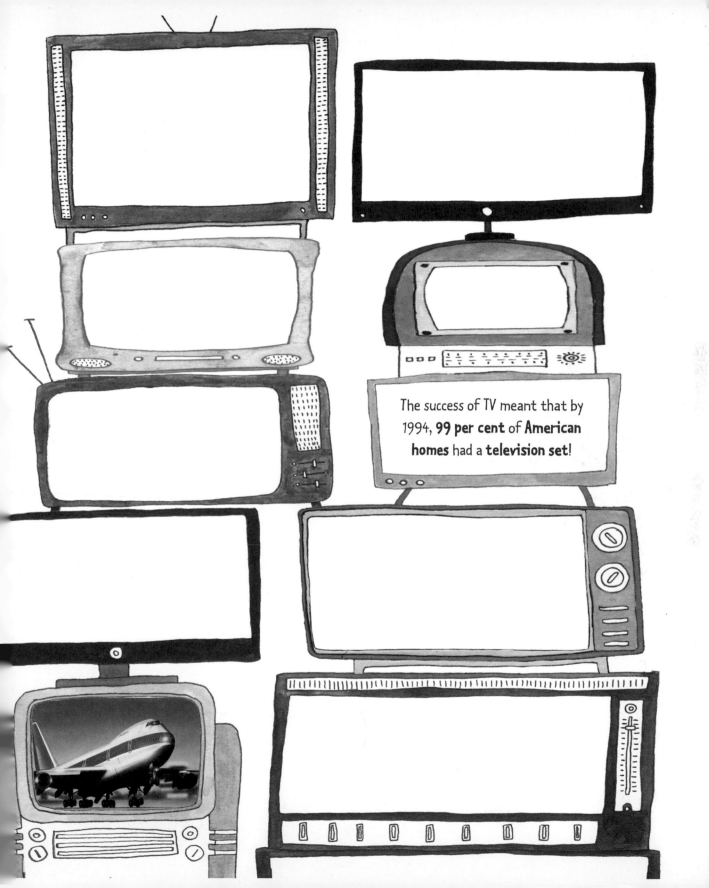

The success of TV meant that by 1994, **99 per cent** of **American homes** had a **television set**!

**COLOUR** ALL
THE VELOCIRAPTOR
DRAWINGS YELLOW

Velociraptor

**COLOUR** ALL THE
BRACHIOSAURUS
DRAWINGS BLUE

Brachiosaurus

Charonosaurus

**COLOUR** ALL
THE CHARONOSAURUS
DRAWINGS RED

The **Brachiosaurus**
weighed up to
**50 tonnes**. That's
the same as
**11 African elephants!**

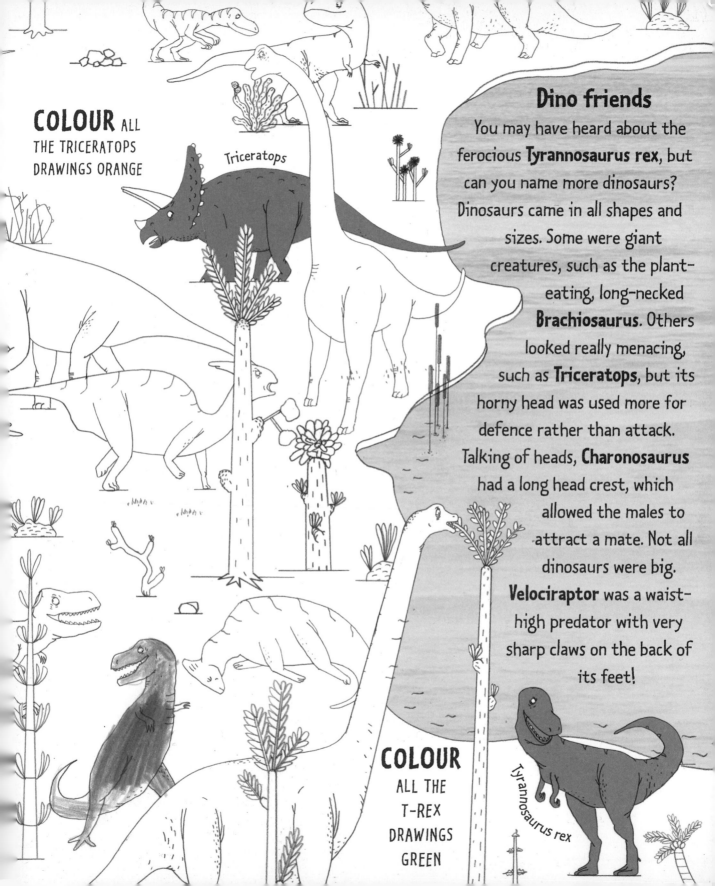

**COLOUR** ALL THE TRICERATOPS DRAWINGS ORANGE

Triceratops

# Dino friends

You may have heard about the ferocious **Tyrannosaurus rex**, but can you name more dinosaurs? Dinosaurs came in all shapes and sizes. Some were giant creatures, such as the plant-eating, long-necked **Brachiosaurus**. Others looked really menacing, such as **Triceratops**, but its horny head was used more for defence rather than attack. Talking of heads, **Charonosaurus** had a long head crest, which allowed the males to attract a mate. Not all dinosaurs were big. **Velociraptor** was a waist-high predator with very sharp claws on the back of its feet!

**COLOUR** ALL THE T-REX DRAWINGS GREEN

Tyrannosaurus rex

COLOUR IN THE PLANETS AND **DRAW** WHAT ELSE YOU THINK IS OUT THERE...

The Sun

Venus

Earth

Mercury

Mars

# Where in the world are we?

Our **solar system** is enormous. Too big to even imagine! It consists of eight **planets**, plus asteroids, moons, dust... the list is almost endless! Everything in our solar system **orbits** around the Sun at different speeds. It takes Earth 365 days to orbit the Sun once, but it takes Neptune nearly 165 years!

The **Sun** is not a planet, but a bi bright **star** situated in the cent of the solar system.

Earth's distance from the Sun means it is neither **too hot**, nor **too cold**. It is the only planet suitable for life (that we know of for now).

Uranus

Neptune

Saturn

Jupiter

**DRAW** A RANGE OF EXPRESSIONS AND FEELINGS

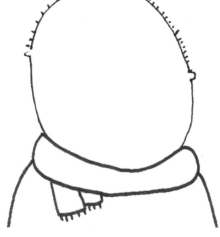

MAKE ME **HAPPY!**

## Face your feelings!

How are you feeling at the moment? Your **facial expression** will probably reveal your current **emotion**. There are many different facial expressions, maybe as many as 5,000! They can be subtle, obvious, and change in an instant. The five key muscles in your face **move** in various directions to turn what you are feeling into an expression.

Fear makes your eyes **widen** to show the whites of your eyes, whereas **anger** makes your eyes **narrow** and glaring.

MAKE ME **ANGRY!**

MAKE ME **SAD!**

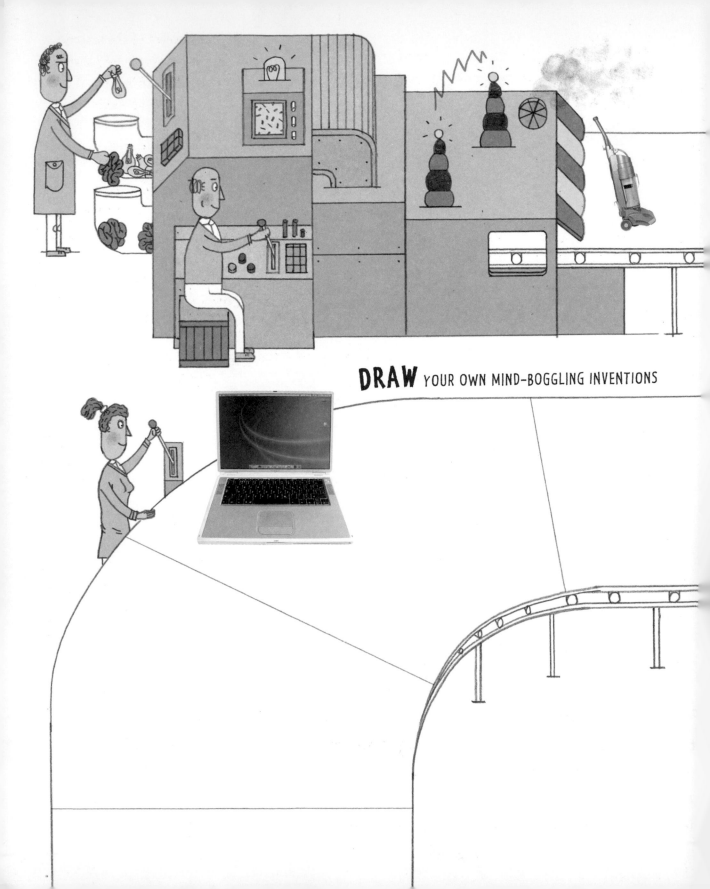

**DRAW** YOUR OWN MIND-BOGGLING INVENTIONS

The development of the **internal combustion engine** in 1859 changed transport forever. The burning of **fuel** in an engine made travel much quicker.

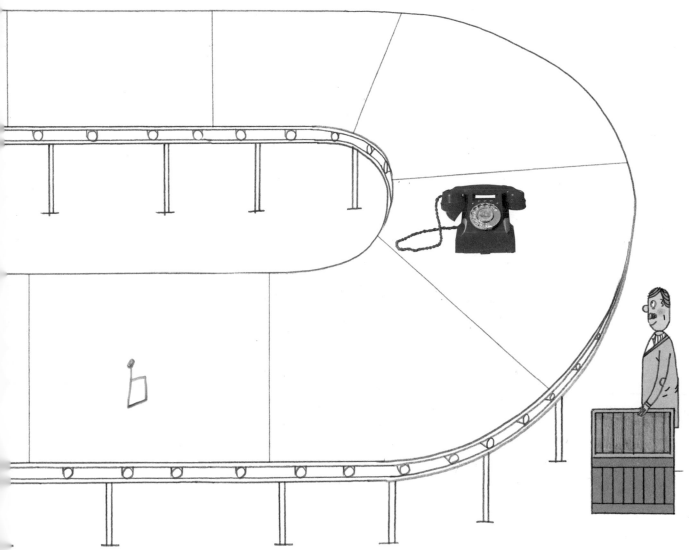

## Eureka!

From wheels to computers, **inventions** continue to change the way we live. Inventors are always trying to improve an invention already in existence, or thinking of something **completely new**. If you think of an invention to help you with your homework or chores, write it down — you could be on to something!

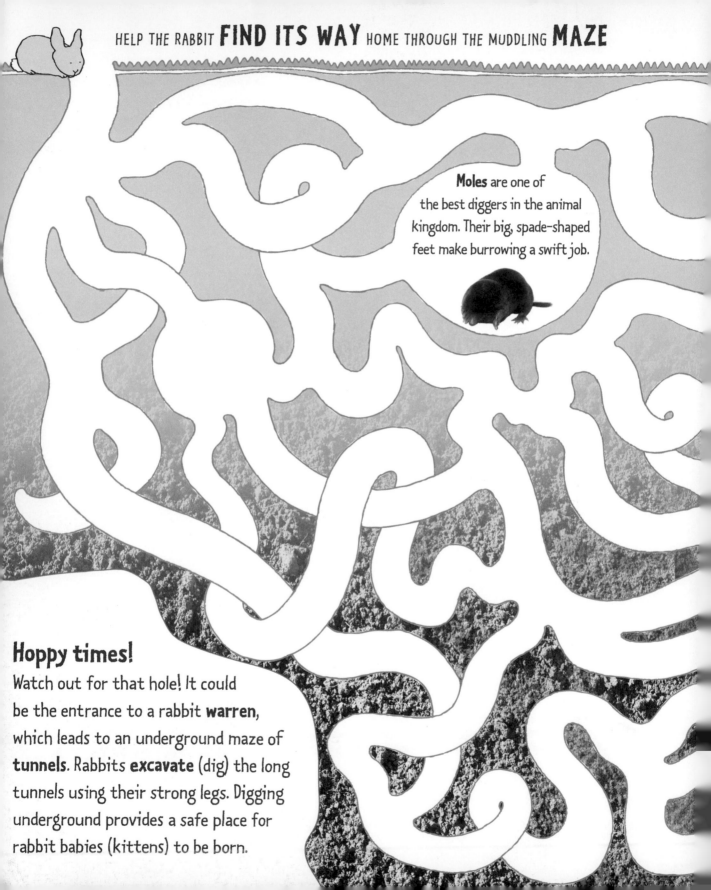

**Moles** are one of the best diggers in the animal kingdom. Their big, spade-shaped feet make burrowing a swift job.

## Hoppy times!

Watch out for that hole! It could be the entrance to a rabbit **warren**, which leads to an underground maze of **tunnels**. Rabbits **excavate** (dig) the long tunnels using their strong legs. Digging underground provides a safe place for rabbit babies (kittens) to be born.

**Foxes** are also good diggers and live in **dens.** They sometimes use an empty rabbit burrow to settle down in.

DRAW MORE UNDERGROUND ANIMALS

# Doodle gallery!

Art has been around for thousands of years, from cave paintings to modern day graffiti art. Art is created to record a moment in time, entertain, and to generate an **emotion**, whether it's happiness, fear, or even anger. Art doesn't just have to be a painting – sculpture, collage, and photographs can all be **works of art**.

**DRAW** YOUR OWN STATUE ON THE PLINTH

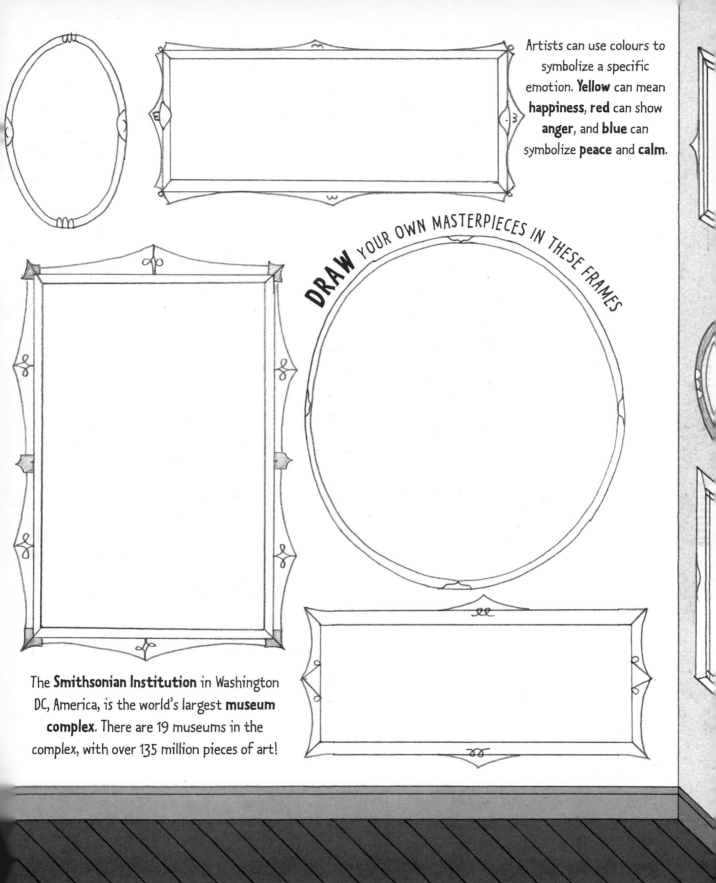

Artists can use colours to symbolize a specific emotion. **Yellow** can mean **happiness**, **red** can show **anger**, and **blue** can symbolize **peace** and **calm**.

DRAW YOUR OWN MASTERPIECES IN THESE FRAMES

The **Smithsonian Institution** in Washington DC, America, is the world's largest **museum complex**. There are 19 museums in the complex, with over 135 million pieces of art!

**DRAW** YOUR OWN WESTERN **MOVIE SCENE...**

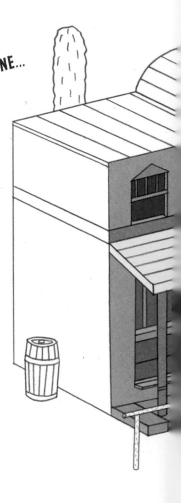

The first western was a **silent film** made in 1903 called *The Great Train Robbery*.

# WANTED

**DRAW** YOUR OWN WESTERN **WANTED POSTER...**

BANK

SALOON

COUNTY JAIL

## Quick on the draw!

A **western** movie is set in the American old west (1850s–1900s). A classic western features a lone **cowboy** fighting for justice, who manages to save a damsel in distress along the way. There is often action in a **frontier town**, with a saloon bar, bank (good for robbing), and jailhouse (where the sheriff rules).

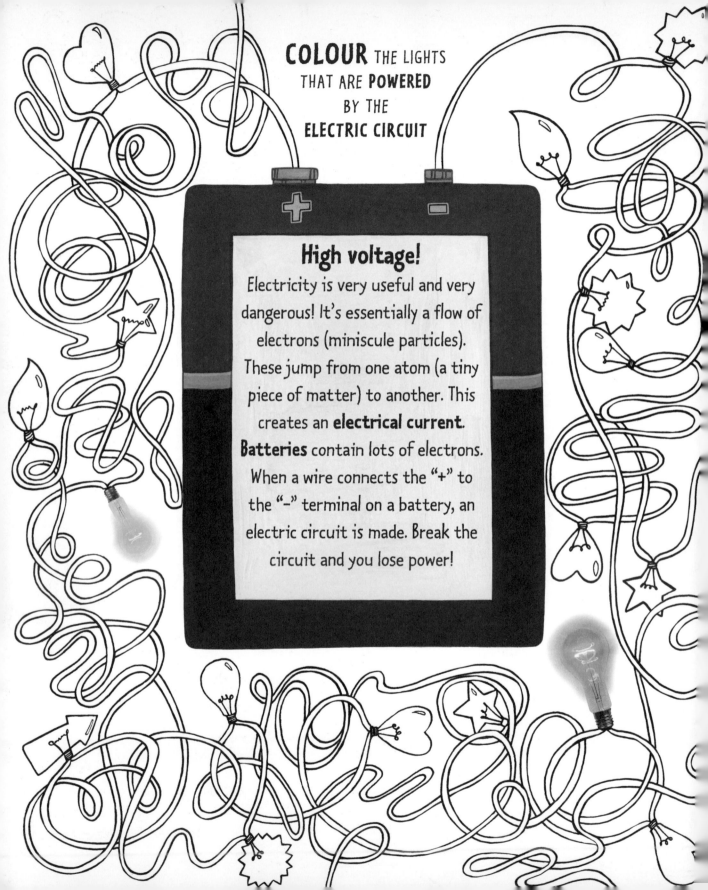

**COLOUR** THE LIGHTS THAT ARE **POWERED** BY THE **ELECTRIC CIRCUIT**

## High voltage!

Electricity is very useful and very dangerous! It's essentially a flow of electrons (miniscule particles). These jump from one atom (a tiny piece of matter) to another. This creates an **electrical current**. **Batteries** contain lots of electrons. When a wire connects the "+" to the "–" terminal on a battery, an electric circuit is made. Break the circuit and you lose power!

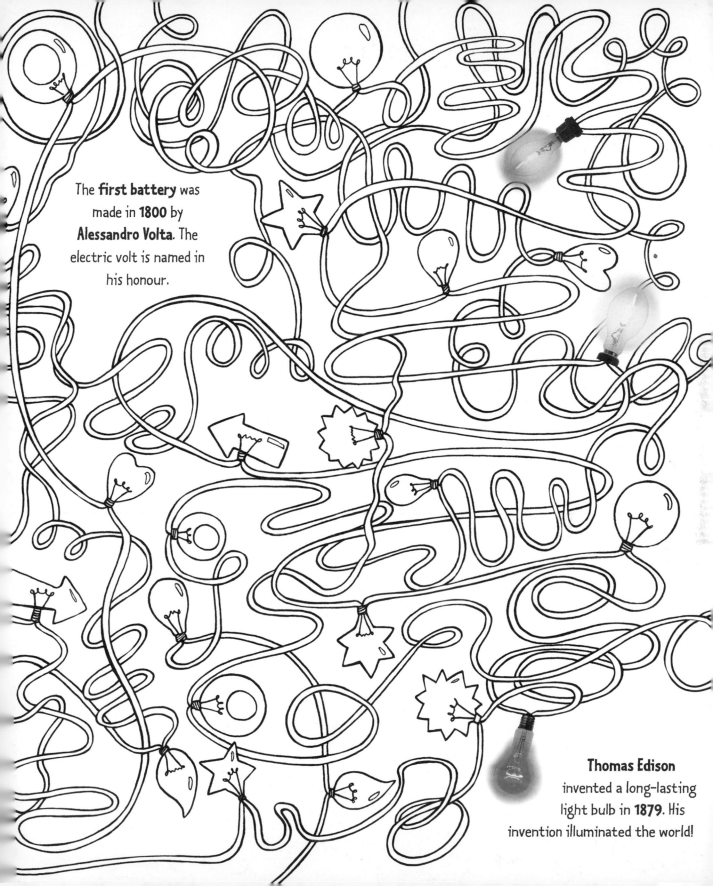

The **first battery** was made in **1800** by **Alessandro Volta**. The electric volt is named in his honour.

**Thomas Edison** invented a long-lasting light bulb in **1879**. His invention illuminated the world!

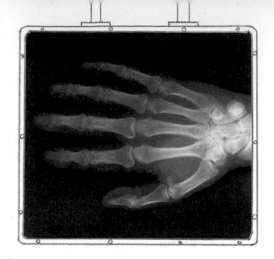

## Not-so-funny bones

Without bones, humans and animals would be like jelly – all wobbly and floppy. The **skeleton** allows us to move around and keeps everything inside the body in place. Bones are made up of **living cells**, which help them to **grow** and to **heal** if anything gets broken.

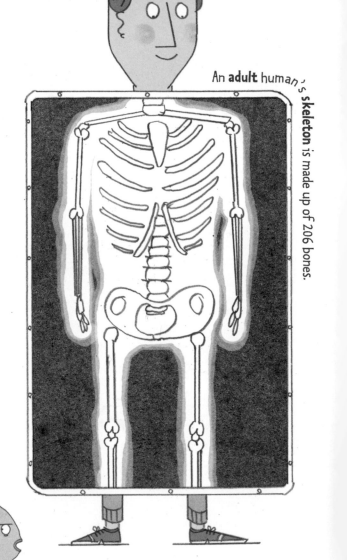

An **adult** human's **skeleton** is made up of 206 bones.

**DRAW** THE SKELETONS OF THESE ANIMALS

An **elephant's skeleton** consists of more than 300 bones. Elephants don't have any bones in their trunk though, only **muscles**.

## Spring ahoy

You are on the side of Earth that is tilting towards the Sun. Birds nest, grass grows, and the **first flowers** start to **bloom**!

## Summer time

Now you are tilted **as far** towards the **Sun** as you'll be all year. All the trees are green and glossy, chicks **fly the nest**, and there are bugs galore.

FINISH **DRAWING** THE DIFFERENT **SEASONS**...

**What season** it is depends on one thing – whether you are tilted **towards** or **away** from the **Sun**. As Earth **spins** around tilted axis, on its **yearly orbit** of the Sun, some regions of Earth are tilted towards the Sun while others are tilted away

## Autumn fall

The side of the Earth you are on is tilting **away** from the **Sun**. Leaves on trees turn red, orange, and brown, and it gets **dark earlier**.

## Winter chill

You are now tilted **away** from the **Sun** so there's **less sunlight**. It is getting colder so animals and insects **hibernate**.

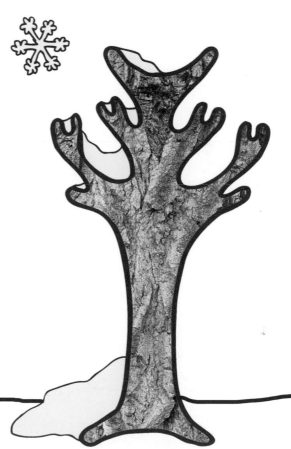

Around the middle of Earth is an **imaginary line** called the **equator**. It receives a constant level of light from the Sun all year round. **Countries** along the **equator** don't have four seasons – just a **dry season** and a **wet season**.

**DRAW** YOUR OWN GHOULISH MOVIE SCENE...

The first horror movie was made in 1896 and was called **Le Manoir du Diable** (The House of the Devil). This **silent short film** was only three minutes long.

## Shock horror!

A **horror movie** features a plot and characters intended to **scare** the life out of the audience. They make a person's **worst nightmare** come true! Although horror movies mostly deal with the **supernatural** (monsters and zombies), they can also feature **baddies** on the loose or an **outbreak** of a deadly disease. Remember to check under the bed at night...

# All aboard!

People have been travelling by **train** since 1825 when the **first public railway** was opened between Stockton and Darlington in the UK. The **track** was just 43 km (27 miles) long. Early trains were powered by a **steam engine**, which was fuelled by **burning coal**. Today, trains are powered by **electricity**.

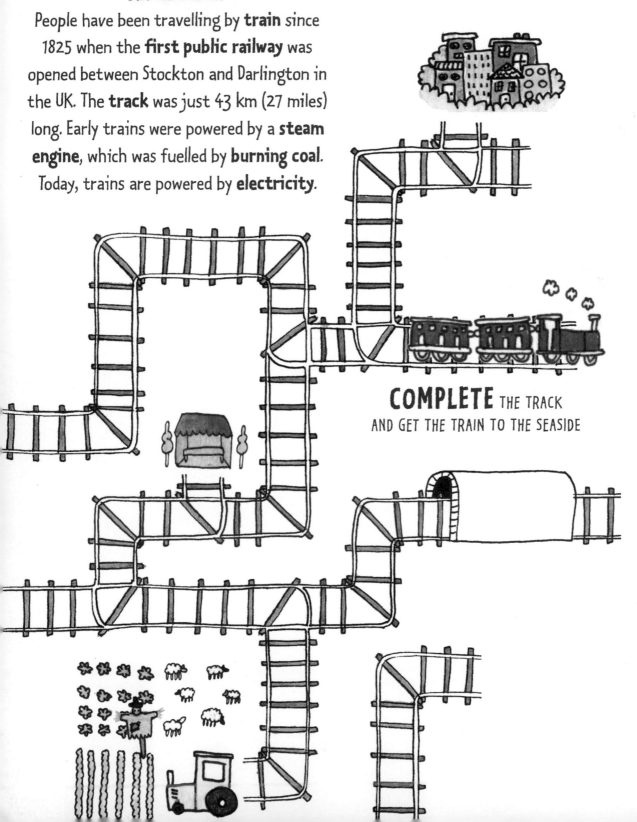

**COMPLETE** THE TRACK
AND GET THE TRAIN TO THE SEASIDE

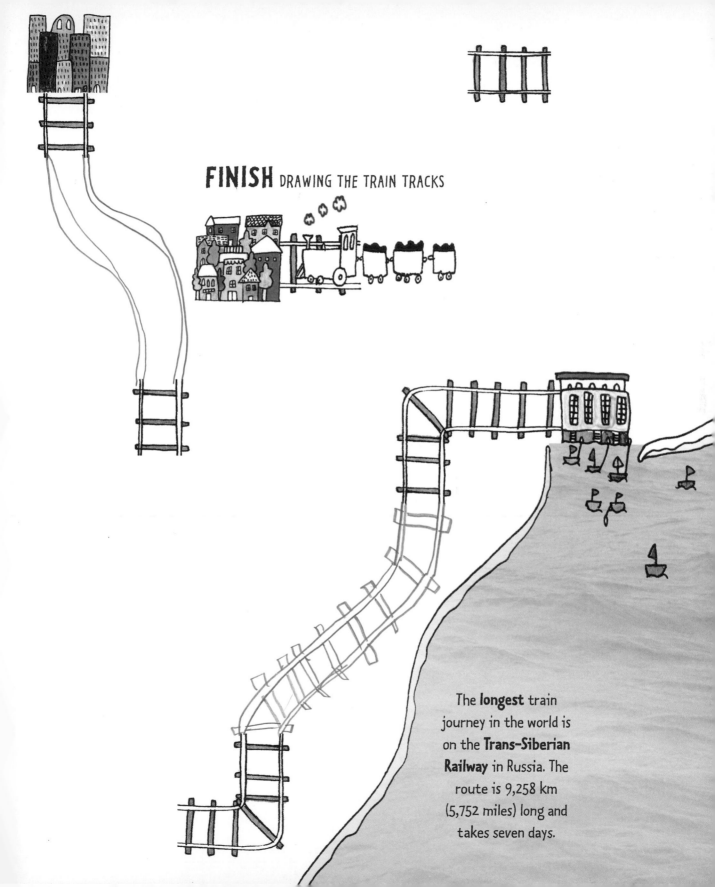

**FINISH** DRAWING THE TRAIN TRACKS

The **longest** train journey in the world is on the **Trans-Siberian Railway** in Russia. The route is 9,258 km (5,752 miles) long and takes seven days.

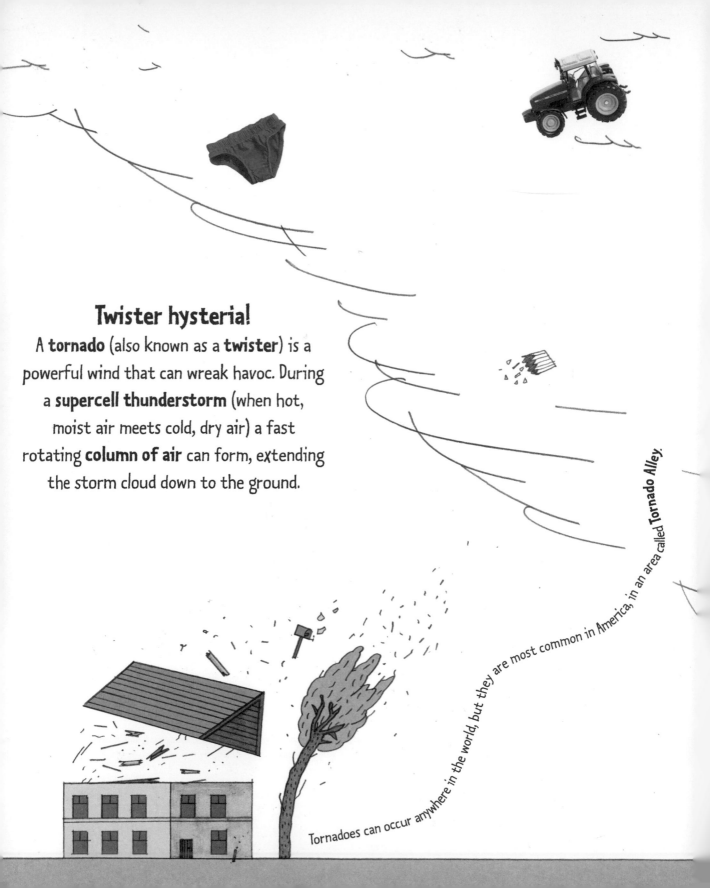

## Twister hysteria!

A **tornado** (also known as a **twister**) is a powerful wind that can wreak havoc. During a **supercell thunderstorm** (when hot, moist air meets cold, dry air) a fast rotating **column of air** can form, extending the storm cloud down to the ground.

Tornadoes can occur anywhere in the world, but they are most common in America, in an area called **Tornado Alley.**

A tornado's **wind speed** can reach more than 480 kph (298 mph) and can pick up anything in its path.

**DRAW** WHAT THE TORNADO HAS WHISKED UP

**FIND** AND **COLOUR** THE CRAFTY CROCS HIDING IN THE SWAMPS

## Happy snappy!

**Crocodiles** are the monsters of the **reptile** world and can grow up to 6 m (20 feet) long. They are ambush hunters and lurk at the water's edge, waiting for an unsuspecting animal to go to the water for a drink. They then propel themselves forward and grab the animal with a snap of their **powerful jaws**.

Crocodiles are **carnivores** (meat eaters) and their diet includes fish, birds, and mammals. Big mammals on the croc menu include zebras, young hippos, big cats and, very occasionally, people!

Women were often considered bad luck on pirate ships, so they had to **dress up as men** to be allowed to climb aboard.

**FINISH** THE PIRATE SHIP AND **DRAW** YOUR OWN PIRATE CREW

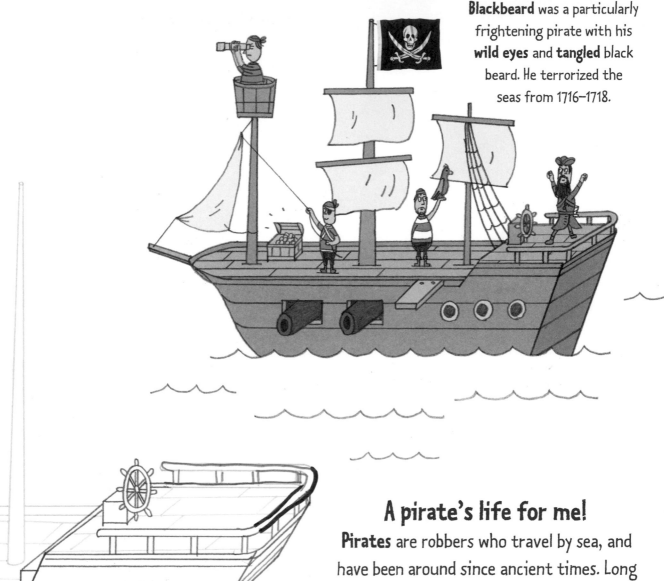

Blackbeard was a particularly frightening pirate with his **wild eyes** and **tangled** black beard. He terrorized the seas from 1716–1718.

## A pirate's life for me!
**Pirates** are robbers who travel by sea, and have been around since ancient times. Long ago, pirates found **riches** galore stealing gold and gems from **Spanish galleons**. Pirates had fearsome reputations, and they advertised this by flying gruesome **flags** high on their mast. Gar ha ha!

**DRAW** THE SHARK'S DINNER **INSIDE** ITS BIG **BELLY**...

·6D S4ARK·

A shark
never needs to visit
the **dentist** because if it **loses**
**a front tooth** or two, a tooth
from the **row** behind moves
**forward** to fill the gap!

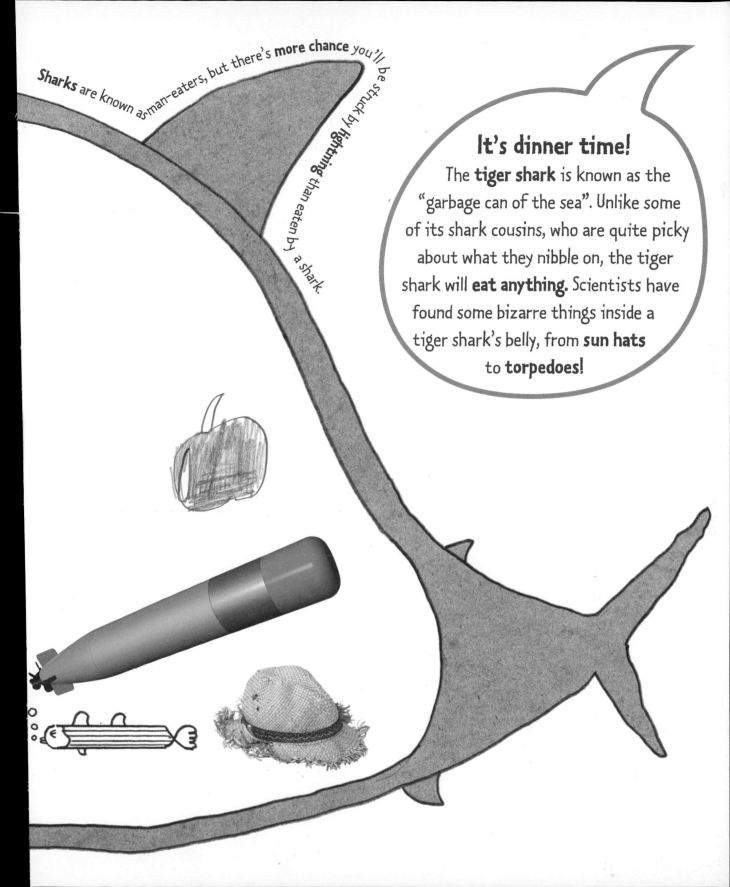

Sharks are known as man-eaters, but there's **more chance** you'll be struck by lightning than eaten by a shark.

### It's dinner time!

The **tiger shark** is known as the "garbage can of the sea". Unlike some of its shark cousins, who are quite picky about what they nibble on, the tiger shark will **eat anything.** Scientists have found some bizarre things inside a tiger shark's belly, from **sun hats** to **torpedoes!**

# Hold on tight!

The exciting (and scary) feeling you get when you are on a roller coaster is caused by **G-force**. As you zoom around the roller coaster, G-force acts on every part of your body, even the organs inside you! The G-force on most roller coasters is up to 4.5 g. A top fighter pilot has to contend with 9 g when performing rapid manoeuvres, and a scientist once survived a rocket-powered sledge ride with a G-force of 46.2 g!

START

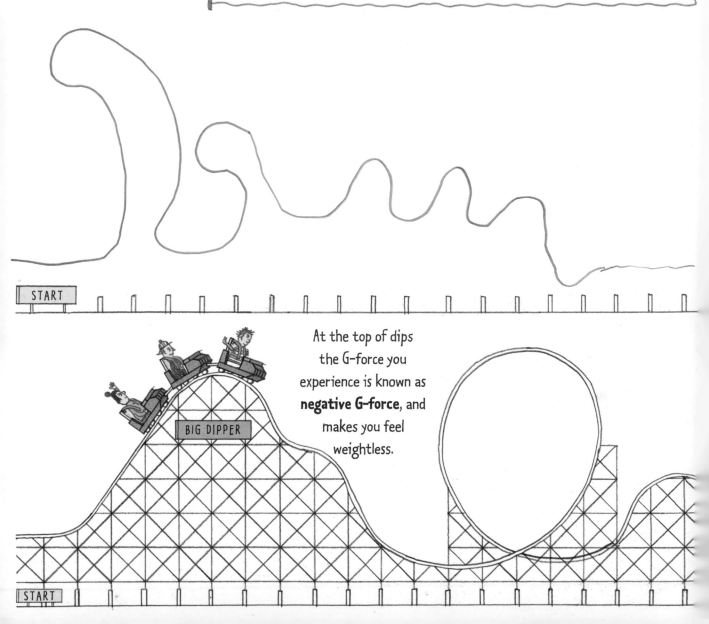

BIG DIPPER

At the top of dips the G-force you experience is known as **negative G-force**, and makes you feel weightless.

START

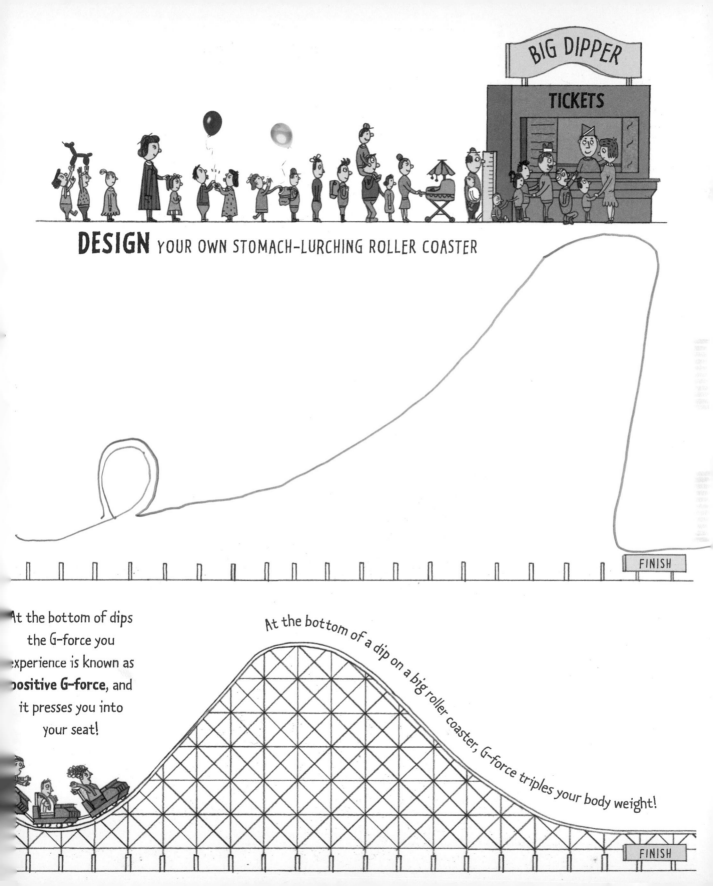

**DESIGN** YOUR OWN STOMACH-LURCHING ROLLER COASTER

BIG DIPPER

TICKETS

FINISH

At the bottom of dips the G-force you experience is known as **positive G-force**, and it presses you into your seat!

At the bottom of a dip on a big roller coaster, G-force triples your body weight!

FINISH

**DRAW** PHOTOS FOR YOUR PHOTO ALBUM

The first photograph was taken by **French inventor** Joseph Nicéphore Niépce in **1826**. The image was of some farm buildings on a sunny day.

## Smile!

Click! Flash! A moment is captured forever by a **camera** when **light** bounces off an object and travels through a camera **lens**, which cleverly arranges the light to form an image. The idea of a camera was first described more than 2,000 years ago when Greek mathematicians and Chinese philosophers described a simple kind of pin-hole camera.

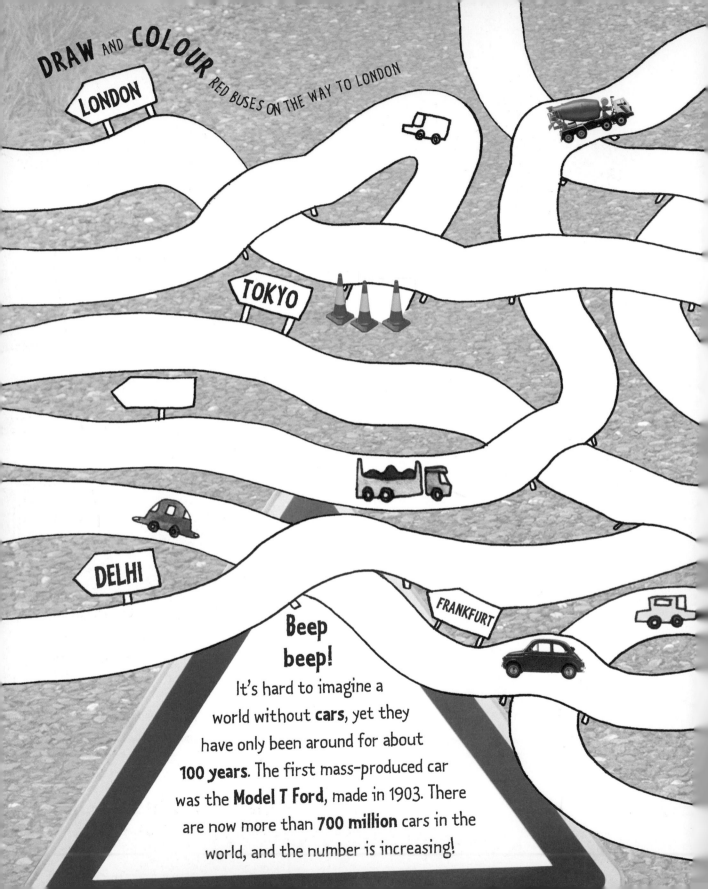

**DRAW** AND **COLOUR** RED BUSES ON THE WAY TO LONDON

LONDON

TOKYO

DELHI

FRANKFURT

## Beep beep!

It's hard to imagine a world without **cars**, yet they have only been around for about **100 years**. The first mass-produced car was the **Model T Ford**, made in 1903. There are now more than **700 million** cars in the world, and the number is increasing!

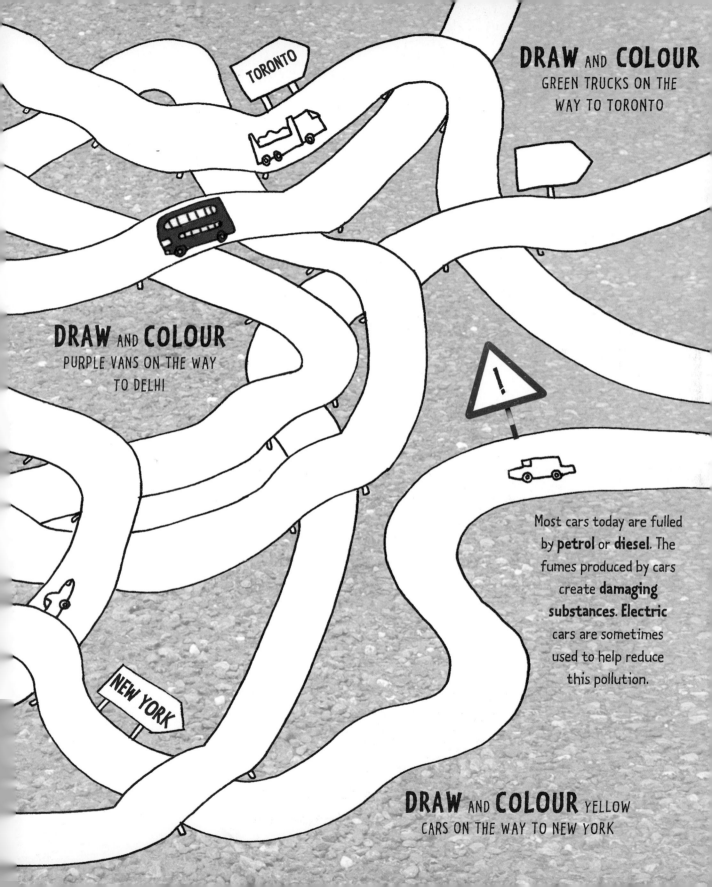

**DRAW** AND **COLOUR**
GREEN TRUCKS ON THE
WAY TO TORONTO

TORONTO

**DRAW** AND **COLOUR**
PURPLE VANS ON THE WAY
TO DELHI

Most cars today are fulled
by **petrol** or **diesel**. The
fumes produced by cars
create **damaging
substances. Electric**
cars are sometimes
used to help reduce
this pollution.

NEW YORK

**DRAW** AND **COLOUR** YELLOW
CARS ON THE WAY TO NEW YORK

# Hungry plants!

Plants that chomp on insects? Yes, we **carnivorous plants** trap and consume yummy insects and other bugs. Carnivorous plants can be **passive** and attract insects with a **sticky sap** or drown them in **pitchers**. Or we can be **active** and actually move to trap our prey. Gotcha!

One deadly plant, **Nepenthes rajah**, is native to the mountains of Borneo. It is so big that it can **trap rats** and **frogs**.

# DRAW YOUR OWN BUG-EATING MONSTER PLANT

The **Venus flytrap** is an active carnivorous plant. It has little **hairs** on its pad-like leaves that sense when an insect has landed. The hairs prompt the trap to **close tightly shut**.

# Space to live!

The **International Space Station** (ISS) is made up of lots of modules joined together and is as big as a **football pitch**. Up to six astronauts can live there, from any of the **16 countries** that helped build the station. It travels around Earth at an average speed of **27,700 kph (17,210 mph)** completing 16 orbits per day!

People have **lived** in the International Space Station **every day** since the **year 2000!**

DESIGN AND **DRAW** YOUR OWN **SPACE STATION**

# Digging for diamonds!

Diamonds are **gemstones** and are very valuable. They form deep below Earth's surface and are made from **carbon**. Diamonds are judged according to the four Cs – **carat** (weight), **clarity**, **colour**, and **cut**. The bigger, clearer, and more sparkly they are, the more expensive!

Natural diamonds are mined from the ground and can take millions of years to form.

They are then cut, using special tools, from a rough stone into a beautiful gem.

Once they are highly polished and sparkly, the diamonds are turned into jewellery.

DRAW YOUR OWN TWINKLING JEWELLERY

## Hello from up here!

The **North Pole** is in the **Arctic**, which is a frozen area of sea at the **top** of the Earth. Polar bears and killer whales can be found in the Arctic. In December, it is **winter**, and the North Pole is dark all day. In June, it is the Arctic summer, and it is **daylight** the entire time – even at night!

NORTH POLE

**DRAW** MORE POLAR BEARS LOOKING FOR THEIR DINNER

NORTH

# Hello from down here!

The **South Pole** is in **Antarctica** and is the coldest place on Earth. Antarctica is a **frozen mountainous continent**, surrounded by ocean, at the **bottom** of the Earth. Penguins and seals live in this frozen land. The Antarctic **winter** is in June, and its **summer** is in December.

**DRAW** MORE PENGUINS HAVING FUN

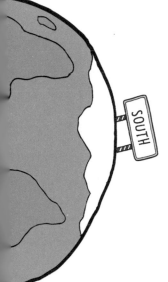

SOUTH

SOUTH POLE

# The shape of things!

Shapes make up our world. Whether it's bicycle wheels (**circles**), a beach towel (**rectangle**), or honeycomb (**hexagons**), everything is made of shapes! Shapes help us build things safely, they allow us to draw fantastic masterpieces, and scientists use them to understand nature!

**COLOUR** THE **OCTAGON** TOWELS **GREEN** AND THE **CIRCLE** TOWELS **BLUE**

octagon (8 sides)

**COLOUR** THE **SQUARE** TOWELS **RED**

**DRAW** A **SPOTTY PATTERN** ON THE **TRIANGLE** TOWELS

triangle (3 side

**Squares** are very tidy. They have four **sides** of the **same length**. Also a square's **corners** are all **right angles** – 90 degrees. When you add up all the angles they equal 360, which is the number of degrees in a circle!

square (4 sides)

rectangle (4 sides)

**DRAW** SUNBATHERS ON THE **RECTANGLE** TOWELS

dodecagon (12 sides)

hexagon (6 sides)

**DECORATE** THE **HEXAGON** UMBRELLAS

**MAKE** THE **DODECAGON** TOWELS STRIPY

**COLOUR** THE **DECAGON** TOWELS **PURPLE**

pentagon (5 sides)

decagon (10 sides)

**DRAW** A STARFISH ON THE **PENTAGON** TOWELS

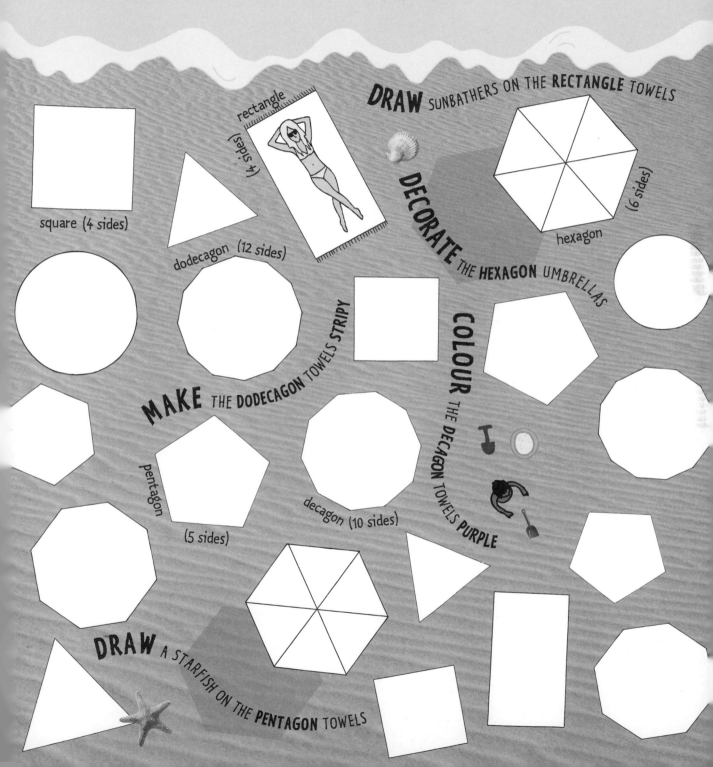

Castles were built for defence. They had **arrow slits** in the walls so archers could safely shoot arrows at the attackers. The gaps at the top of the walls, called **crenellations**, enabled the defenders to drop heavy stones on the enemy below.

# Charge the castle!

Well, try to charge. Medieval castles were fortresses designed to protect the people that lived inside from enemy attack. Most had a **moat** with a **drawbridge**, **thick walls**, and a **keep**. The keep was the highest, strongest, most secure place in the castle. Stay out and keep out!

Knights lived inside the castle. They would wear a suit of **heavy armour** to go into battle.

# Seeing things?

Have you ever gazed at clouds and seen one shaped like a tortoise? Or maybe you saw something out of the corner of your eye that wasn't there? Humans have evolved the skill to interpret **visual data** and compare it to things from **memory**. This skill was useful when we were hunter-gatherers and spotting a bear in the bushes was a matter or life or lunch!

COLOUR IN WHAT YOU SEE IN THE CLOUDS

The part of the brain where these visual conclusions are made is called the **ventral fusiform cortex**, also known as the fusiform face area.

Octopuses found in coral reefs live in **dens**. When they feel threatened, octopuses squirt **black ink** to confuse the predator, giving the octopus time to escape.

The world's **largest** coral reef is the **Great Barrier Reef** on the east coast of Australia. It's so big that it can be seen from outer space!

# Under the sea!

Called the "rainforests of the sea", **coral reefs** are found underwater and are home to millions of marine animals, including fish, turtles, and sea snakes. Although coral looks like plants and rocks, it is actually made of tiny animals, called **polyps**.

DRAW AND COLOUR THE BEAUTIFUL CORAL REEF AND ITS INHABITANTS

# A web of flies!

Spiders spin **webs** with one thing in mind – to catch dinner! A spider's web is made from **silk** produced from a spider's **spinneret glands**. A spider will weave its sticky web and wait for its prey to become entangled. Once something is trapped, the spider will rush over and **wrap it up tightly**, ready to eat later.

DRAW WHAT THE SPIDER HAS CAUGHT ON ITS WEB

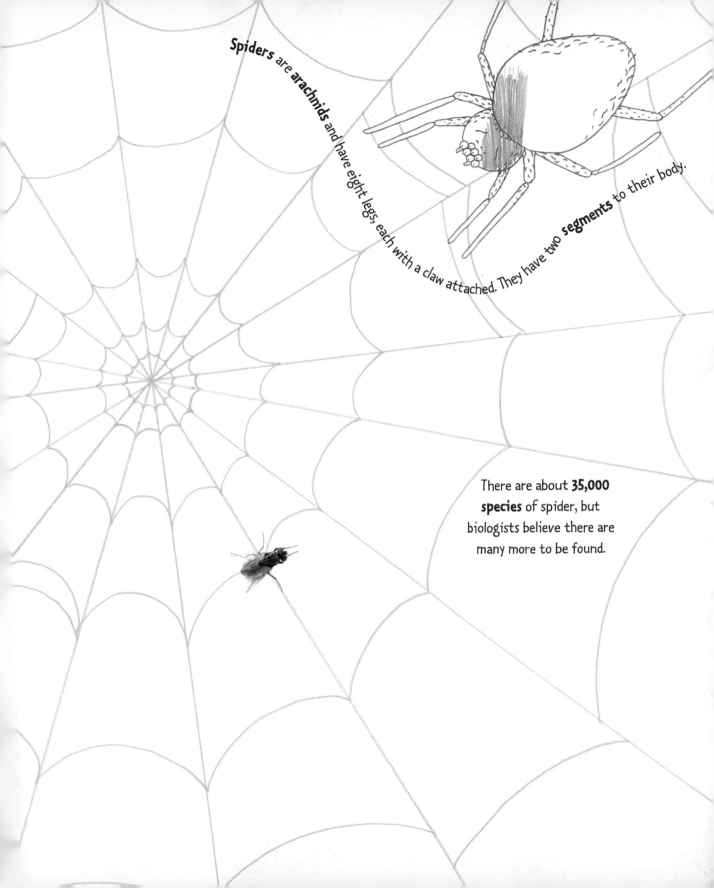

Spiders are **arachnids** and have eight legs, each with a claw attached. They have two **segments** to their body.

There are about **35,000 species** of spider, but biologists believe there are many more to be found.

# Blowing your top!

**Volcanoes** are openings in Earth's rocky crust where **molten rock** bursts and explodes out. As well as erupting molten rock called **lava**, some volcanoes also blow out huge clouds of **ash** and throw out large, round rocks called bombs.

After an eruption, the released lava cools down and creates new rock, including:

**Pumice** rock contains lots of bubbles created by volcanic gases. All these bubbles make the rock really light so it floats in water!

**Basalt** rock is dark and very hard. It is the most common of all volcanic rocks, and can be found everywhere from the ocean floor to the Moon!

DRAW YOUR OWN ERUPTING VOLCANOES

# What a tangle of snakes!

Snakes are known as "slippery creatures", however, **snakeskin** is actually dry. A snake's skin is made up of lots of **scales**, which can be grainy or smooth. When a snake grows it gets too big for its skin. The snake then **sheds** its skin – and it all comes off in one go!

**COLOUR** US IN. WE WON'T BITE... HISS!

# Wall art!

In the beginning, early humans found a way to tell stories using art. But they didn't have paper so they used cave walls! Cave paintings have been found all over the world. The earliest known cave paintings date from 33,000 BCE and were painted onto the walls of the Chauvet caves in France. The cave artists used their fingers, twigs, or leaves as brushes, and made paint from different coloured earth, ash, and berries.

Some cave artists didn't use paints. Instead, they would **scratch away** the top **surface** of the cave to reveal a **lighter rock** underneath.

Men were drawn as **stick men**, but animals were more carefully drawn and coloured in.

DRAW YOUR OWN STORIES ON THE CAVE WALL...

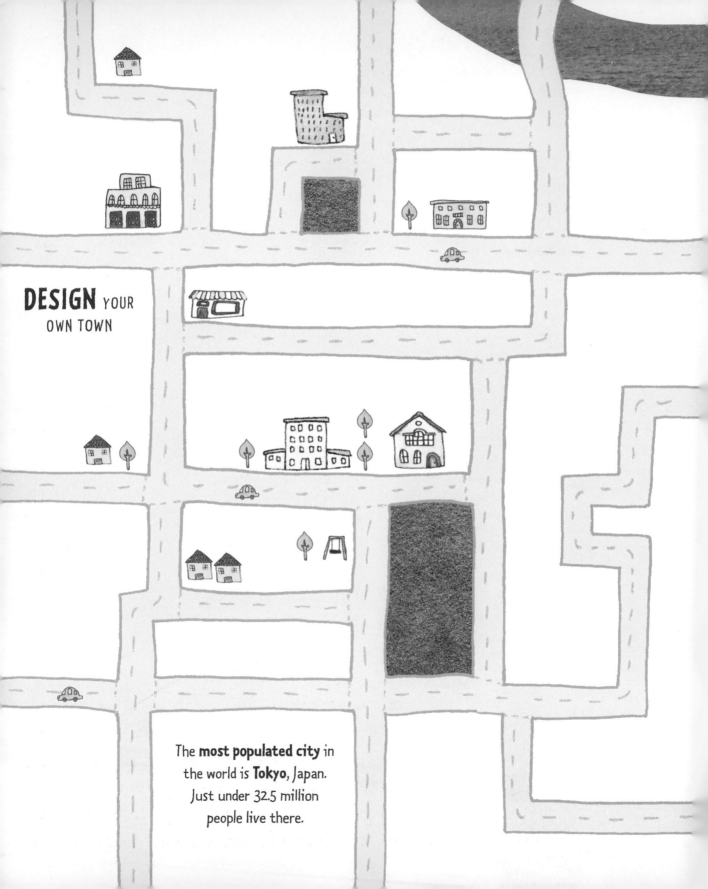

# DESIGN YOUR OWN TOWN

The **most populated city** in
the world is **Tokyo**, Japan.
Just under 32.5 million
people live there.

More than half of the world's population lives in towns and cities.

## KEY

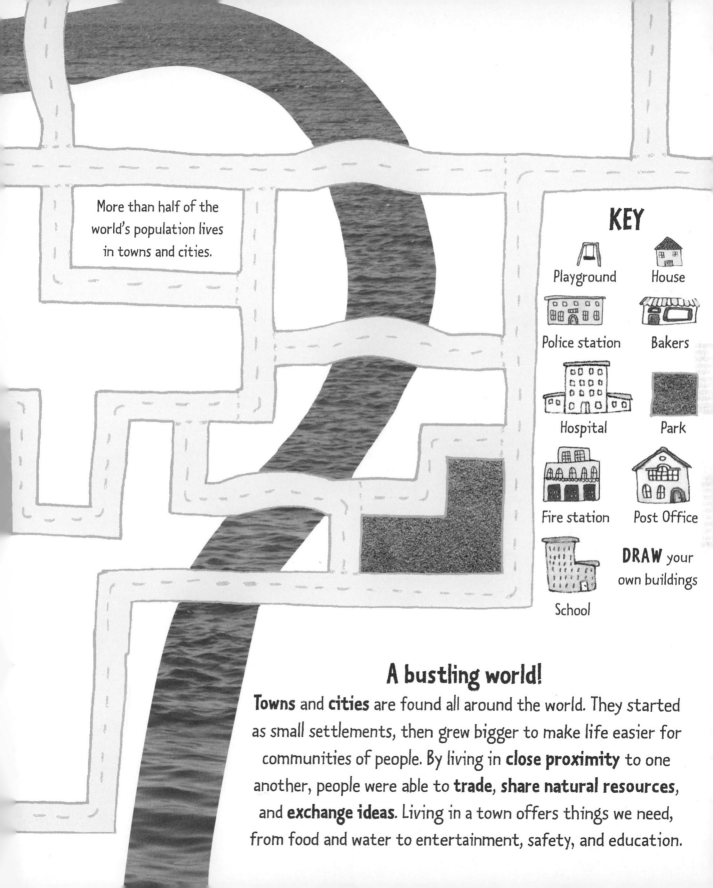

Playground

House

Police station

Bakers

Hospital

Park

Fire station

Post Office

**DRAW** your own buildings

School

# A bustling world!

**Towns** and **cities** are found all around the world. They started as small settlements, then grew bigger to make life easier for communities of people. By living in **close proximity** to one another, people were able to **trade**, **share natural resources**, and **exchange ideas**. Living in a town offers things we need, from food and water to entertainment, safety, and education.

Many people claim to have spotted **UFOs** (unidentified flying objects) in the sky, but no claim has ever been proved to be true.

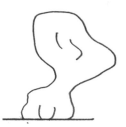
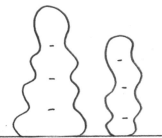

**DRAW** YOUR OWN SCI-FI **MOVIE SCENE...**

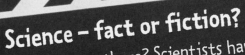

## Science – fact or fiction?

Is there anybody out there? Scientists have long speculated about the existence of things like **aliens** and **time travel**. No one knows if these things are possible so it's left to film makers to imagine what it would be like if they were. **Science fiction** films (sci-fi) are based on science, often futuristic, and look at what would happen if aliens paid us a visit.

The symmetry of butterfly wings is known as **mirror symmetry**.

Butterfly wings are covered in tiny **scales**.

# Spot those wings of symmetry!

Butterflies have beautiful and colourful wings that have **identical patterns**. If you could fold a butterfly in half down its body, its wings would match perfectly. This is **symmetry**.

CAN YOU **MAKE** ALL THE **BUTTERFLIES SYMMETRICAL?**

**COLOUR** US IN!

# That sinking feeling!

Why might an apple **float**, but a pear **sink**? It all depends on the **weight** of the object and its **volume** (how much space it takes up). When an object is placed into water, the water has to move to make room for the object. This is called **displacement**. An object will **sink** because it's **heavier than the water** it has displaced. It will **float** if it weighs **less than the displaced water**.

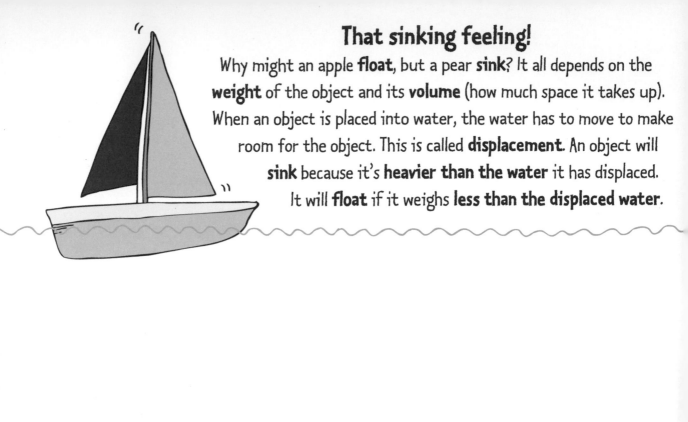

A **cargo ship** is enormous, so why doesn't it sink? The ship's hull is **full of air**, so when the ship is launched into water, the **volume of water displaced is heavier than the ship**, so the ship floats.

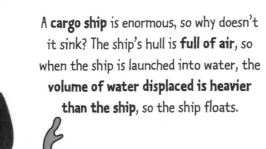

The **physicist Archimedes** is believed to have discovered displacement when he sat in the bath, causing him to shout **"Eureka!"**

**DRAW** MORE THINGS THAT FLOAT OR SINK

**SCRIBBLE** CRAZY AND COOL **HAIRSTYLES** FOR THESE CHILLY-HEADED CHARACTERS...

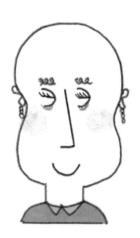 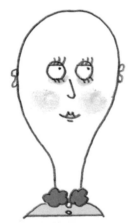 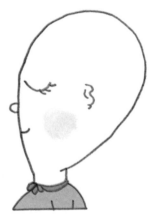

... AND MAYBE SOME **MOUSTACHES** AND **BEARDS**...

... HOW ABOUT SOME **NASAL HAIR** (THAT'S THE HAIR IN YOUR NOSE)?...

... WHY NOT GO MAD AND **SCRIBBLE** SOME **EAR HAIR?**

**Hair-raising stuff!** Hair is an amazing thing, and it's not just there to look good. Hair keeps you warm, protects parts of your body, and even keeps you clean. Hair will grow all over your body, except on your lips, palms of your hands, and soles of your feet.

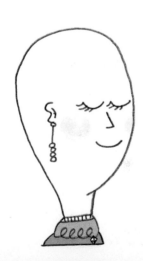

A **man** has about **5,000,000** hair follicles (where hair attaches to your skin) all over **his body!**

**DRAW** ALL THE **JUNK** THAT IS **ORBITING** EARTH

An early piece of **rubbish** that floated in orbit was from the first American **space-walk**, when astronaut **Ed White** lost his **glove**!

## No space for rubbish!
We are careful about throwing things away on Earth, but what about in space? At present there is a jungle of **debris orbiting our planet**, from broken satellites to the remains of astronauts' lunch boxes. It's getting so crowded that the International Space Station has to dodge large chunks of debris as it orbits Earth!

## On safari!

Shh! Keep very quiet! A **safari** is an overland journey usually across **Africa's grasslands**. It will bring you up close to the most amazing animals in the world. Africa is home to huge **herds** of **grazers**, such as **zebras**. They are hunted by **lions** and other **big cats**. **Scavengers**, such as **vultures**, clean up any leftovers.

A group of lions is called a **pride**. There can be up to 40 lions in one pride.

Many **safari animals** are in danger from **hunters**. Throughout Africa, **conservation movements** are in place to **protect** the animals.

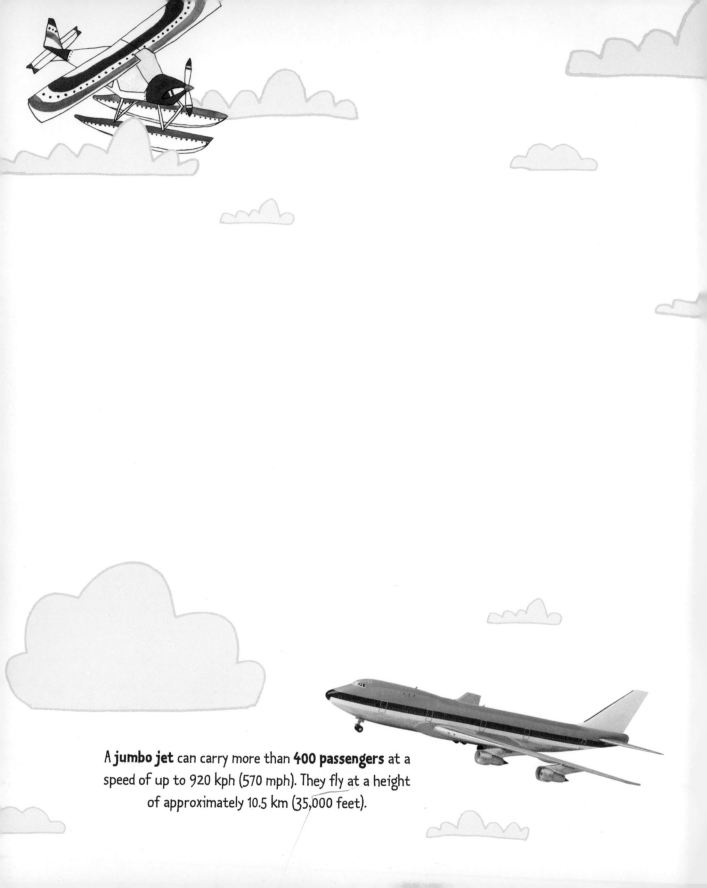

A **jumbo jet** can carry more than **400 passengers** at a speed of up to 920 kph (570 mph). They fly at a height of approximately 10.5 km (35,000 feet).

## Is it a bird?

Aeroplanes are heavy, so how do they stay in the sky? The engine and propeller create a forward force call **thrust**. This moves air over the wings creating an upwards force called **lift**. Both **thrust and lift** must be **greater** than the opposing forces of **drag and weight** for the aeroplane to fly.

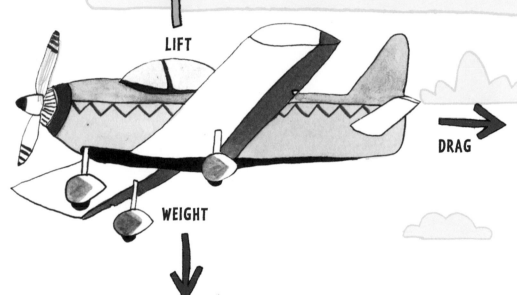

LIFT

THRUST

DRAG

WEIGHT

**DESIGN** YOUR OWN AIRCRAFT!

# We are family

**Arthropods** make up 90 per cent of all animal species in the world. There are four types of arthropods: **insects** (including dragonflies and beetles), **arachnids** (including spiders and scorpions), water-loving **crustaceans** (including crabs and lobsters), and **"-pedes"** (including centipedes and millipedes). Arthropods have **segmented bodies** (made up of more than one part) and are **cold-blooded** (they take on the temperature of their surroundings).

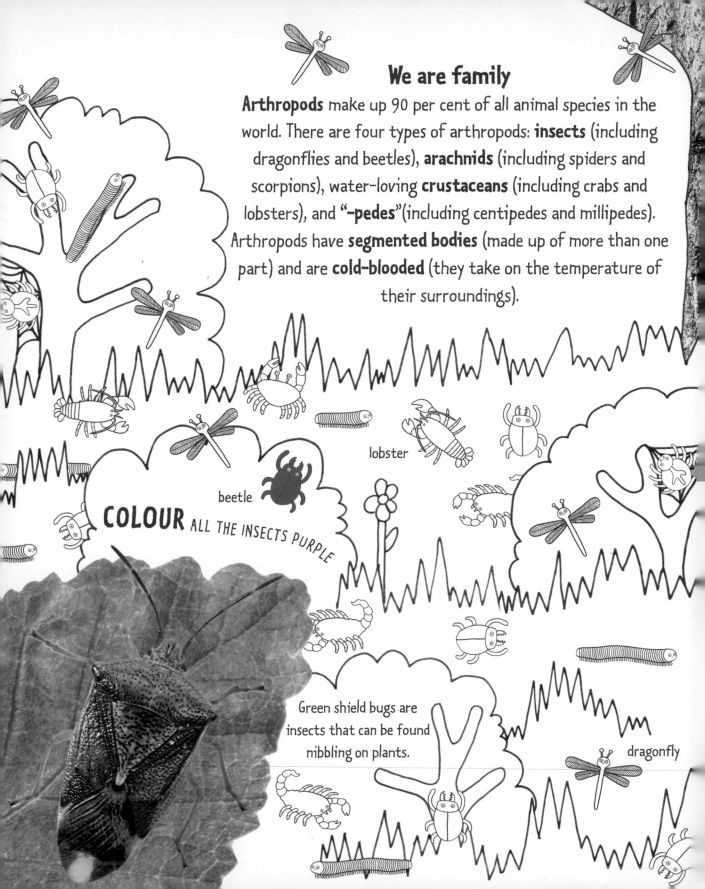

**COLOUR** ALL THE INSECTS PURPLE

beetle

lobster

Green shield bugs are insects that can be found nibbling on plants.

dragonfly

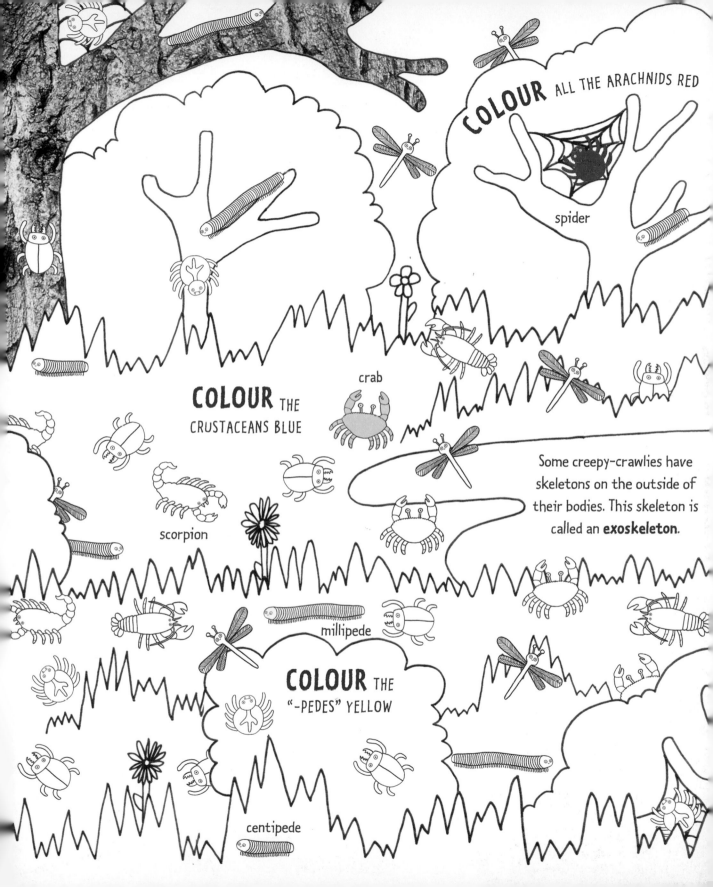

**COLOUR** ALL THE ARACHNIDS RED

spider

**COLOUR** THE
CRUSTACEANS BLUE

crab

scorpion

Some creepy-crawlies have
skeletons on the outside of
their bodies. This skeleton is
called an **exoskeleton**.

millipede

**COLOUR** THE
"-PEDES" YELLOW

centipede

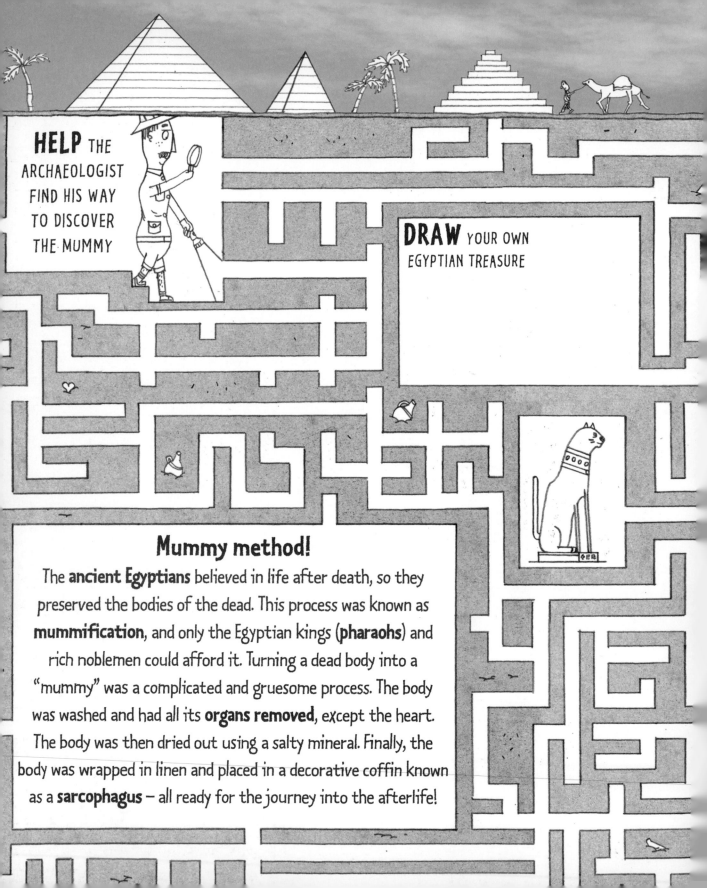

**HELP** THE ARCHAEOLOGIST FIND HIS WAY TO DISCOVER THE MUMMY

**DRAW** YOUR OWN EGYPTIAN TREASURE

## Mummy method!

The **ancient Egyptians** believed in life after death, so they preserved the bodies of the dead. This process was known as **mummification**, and only the Egyptian kings (**pharaohs**) and rich noblemen could afford it. Turning a dead body into a "mummy" was a complicated and gruesome process. The body was washed and had all its **organs removed**, except the heart. The body was then dried out using a salty mineral. Finally, the body was wrapped in linen and placed in a decorative coffin known as a **sarcophagus** – all ready for the journey into the afterlife!

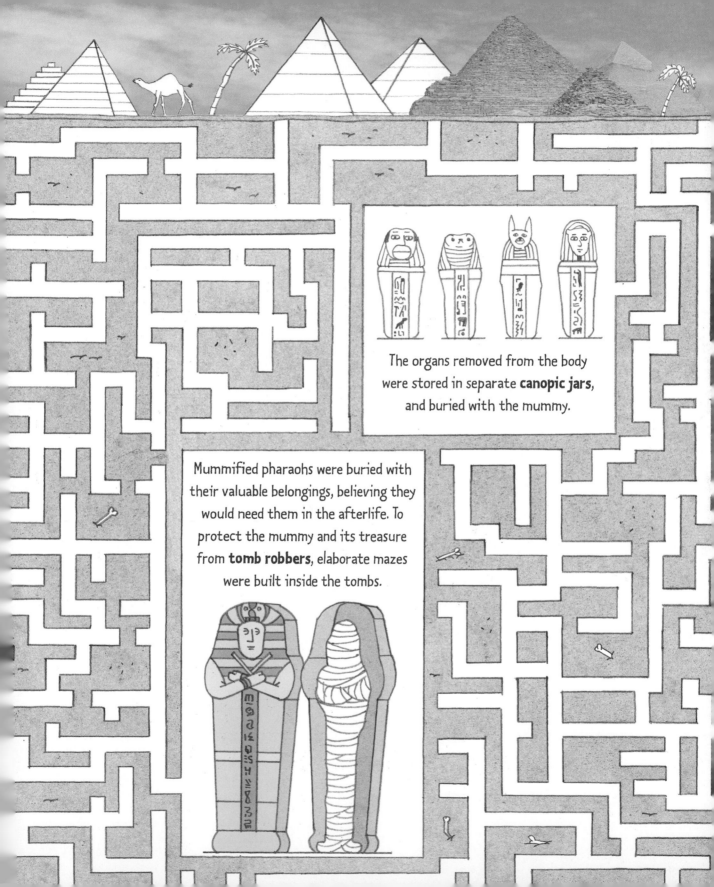

The organs removed from the body were stored in separate **canopic jars**, and buried with the mummy.

Mummified pharaohs were buried with their valuable belongings, believing they would need them in the afterlife. To protect the mummy and its treasure from **tomb robbers**, elaborate mazes were built inside the tombs.

# If you go down to the woods today...

Most people have heard of rainforests, but what about **temperate deciduous forests?** Here the trees grow in cool, rainy areas and consist of trees that lose their leaves in the autumn, but regrow them in spring. Many well-known animals live in these forests, including squirrels, bears, deer, and owls.

**DRAW** YOUR OWN FOREST SCENE

The **American black bear** is a large bear that can grow up to 1.8 m (6 ft) long. It uses its **sharp claws** to help it climb trees and reach yummy fruit.

In the cold winter months, certain animals, such as squirrels, **hibernate**. This means they go into a very deep sleep and wake up when it's warmer.

# You, Robot!

**Robots** sound like something from a movie, but they are actually part of our lives today. Factories and businesses use robots to make things, doctors use them to **help in operations**, and scientists use them to **explore** places too dangerous for humans to go, such as Mars!

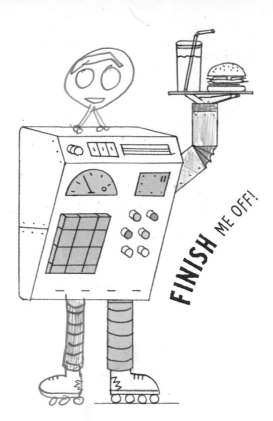

**DESIGN** YOUR OWN FUTURISTIC **ROBOTS!**

FINISH ME OFF!

Kymani

Hi, I'm a hosting robot. You can hire me to host a party or event.

The bright colours produced by a firework are created by the metallic chemical inside it. **Copper** makes **blue** and **sodium** makes **yellow**.

## Bang! Pop! Whizz!

Oooh! Ahh! **Fireworks** consist of **gunpowder** and different **metallic chemicals**, such as copper and sodium, wrapped up tightly in a paper tube with a **fuse**. Once the fuse is lit, the firework shoots high into the sky, and becomes hot making all the chemicals **explode**, releasing their **energy** as **light**, **heat**, and **sound**.

FINISH AND COLOUR YOUR OWN SPECTACULAR FIREWORKS DISPLAY

**DRAW** MORE BUSY BEES VISITING THE FLOWERS

Bees are attracted to **bright, sweet-smelling** flowers. They drink the sugary **nectar** produced by the flower.

**FINISH** AND **COLOUR** THE GARDEN

## DON'T BUZZ OFF!

On a hot sunny day, buzzing bees can seem like a pain, especially if you get stung! But in fact bees are very important insects and vital for all plants. Bees are **pollinators and help plants reproduce**. When a bee lands on a flower to feed, the flower's **pollen** sticks to the bee's body, so when the bee lands on another flower, the pollen falls off and fertilizes the plant.

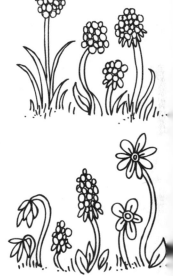

here are around **20,000** known species of bee in the world.

# Flying high!

Birds make flying look so easy. How hard can it be? For many centuries humans have tried to **fly like birds**. Early experiments included building "wings" made of **feathers** or a **light-weight wood** that were attached to a brave volunteer. But no matter how much the person flapped his arms, he was unable to fly. Recent inventions include **jet packs** (or rocket packs), which lift the pilot off the ground vertically.

Astronauts on the International Space Station wear small rocket packs called **"SAFER"**. The astronauts use the packs in an emergency if they become detached from the station.

**DRAW** YOUR OWN FLYING MACHINE

**COLOUR** THE SLAVES BLUE

FIND THE EMPEROR WATCHING HIS SUBJECTS AND WEARING HIS WREATH. **COLOUR** HIM PURPLE

**COLOUR** ALL THE GLADIATORS YELLOW

## Romans rule!

**Ancient Rome** began as a group of small villages, and over several centuries grew into a **powerful empire**. Who was part of this mighty empire? It was ruled by an **emperor** who made all the important decisions. These decisions were advised by the **consuls**, who were similar to today's **politicians**. Roman **gladiators** provided the noblemen with **entertainment**, by fighting each other and wild animals to the death in huge arenas, such as the **Colosseum**. All the hard work was performed by **slaves**, who were mostly prisoners captured by the Roman army.

COLOUR ALL THE CONSULS RED

The Roman Empire created many things we still use today. **Roads**, **concrete**, and our **calendar** were all developed by the Romans.

**Who's a pretty bird then!**

More than 1,500 species of birds live in the **Amazon rainforest** – that's one-third of all bird species in the world! This includes bright and vibrant birds such as **toucans** and **macaws**. The toucan's 19 cm (8 in) long colourful **beak** (bill), is useful for reaching and catching tasty fruit and bugs. Beautiful macaws are parrots and have powerful beaks that easily crack nuts and seeds.

Despite its impressive size, the toucan's beak is not very strong. It is made from a substance called **keratin** (the same substance that humans' nails and hair is made from), and is used to **intimidate** predators, rather than fight them.

**COLOUR** THE RAINFOREST BIRDS

**DRAW** SOMETHING
**FANTASTIC**
TO FINISH THE SECTION.

TURN THE PAGE FOR...

# DOODLEPEDIA
# DINOSAURS

# DOODLEPEDIA
# DINOSAURS

# What is a dinosaur?

Long before humans existed, dinosaurs ruled the Earth. For millions of years these amazing reptiles thrived. Dinosaurs came in all shapes and sizes, and there's still so much we don't know about them. In fact, it's very likely there are new and interesting species we haven't even discovered yet. One thing is for sure though – they were all amazing!

Dinosaurs can be split into two categories: **ornithischians** (bird-hipped), and **saurischians** (lizard-hipped).

They all had **scaly skin,** but some of them also had **feathers.**

**DESIGN** YOUR OWN DINOSAURS.

Most dinosaurs ate plan but many were **meat-ea**

Many dinosaurs were huge,
others were small.

Some walked on **two legs,**
others walked on **four.**

All dinosaurs had **tails.**

All dinosaurs had **clawed or hooved** hands and feet.

# The Mesozoic world

If you travelled back in time to see the rise of the dinosaurs, you'd need to go back about 250 million years to a period of Earth's history called the **Mesozoic Era**. Back then, the Earth was **very different**, and all of the continents were joined together in one big super-continent called **Pangaea**, which means "All Earth". The Mesozoic Era was divided into three periods: the Triassic, the Jurassic, and the Cretaceous. Each of these periods had its own climate and wildlife.

Because the Mesozoic era was so long, dinosaurs from different periods would have **never met**. In fact, more time separates Stegosaurus from T. rex, than T. rex from us!

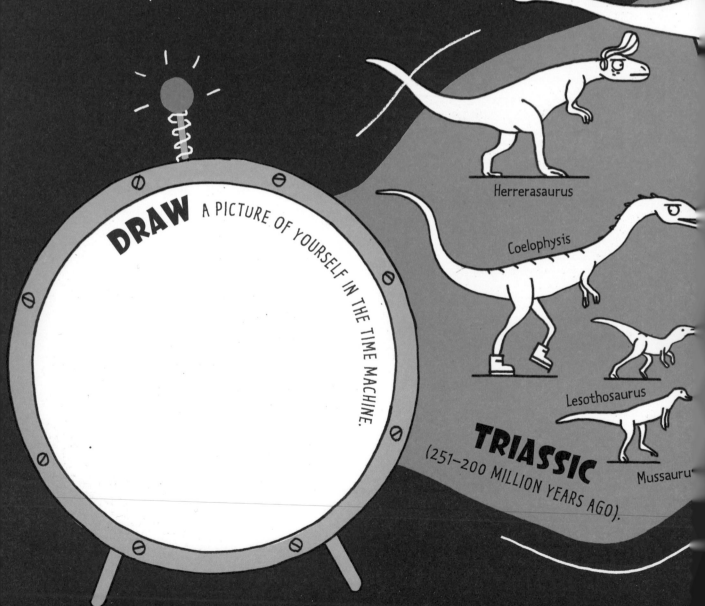

DRAW A PICTURE OF YOURSELF IN THE TIME MACHINE.

Herrerasaurus

Coelophysis

Lesothosaurus

Mussauru*

**TRIASSIC**
(251–200 MILLION YEARS AGO).

Pterodactylus

Oviraptor

Velociraptor

HUMANS
65 MILLION YEARS
IN THE FUTURE.

Pachycephalosaurus

Brachiosaurus

**COLOUR**
ALL THE DINOSAURS.

Tyrannosaurus rex
(T. rex)

Triceratops

Stegosaurus

Spinosaurus

Eoraptor

Iguanodon

**CRETACEOUS**
(145–65 MILLION YEARS AGO).

**JURASSIC** (200–145 MILLION YEARS AGO).

The Earth was very **dry** during the Triassic period. Only the coast and valleys saw much water.

# FINISH THE REST
## OF THE TRIASSIC SCENE.

Herrerasaurus

Eoraptor

GRRR

We don't have any photos to show us what life was like back then. Everything we know, we learn from **studying the remains** of prehistoric things (fossils).

Plateosaurus

# The Triassic period

The Earth's scenery was very different during the **Triassic period** (between 251–200 million years ago). It was very hot and the land was covered in large patches of desert, with no grass or flowers, and only a few plants. It was during the early Triassic period that the first dinosaurs, such as the Eoraptor **(EE-oh-rap-tor)**, Plateosaurus **(PLATE-ee-oh-SORE-us)**, and Herrerasaurus **(her-RARE-uh-SAWR-us)** first emerged.

# The Jurassic period

By the time the Triassic period ended 200 million years ago, the Earth had **changed dramatically**. The supercontinent Pangaea **split apart**, creating new continents, oceans, and seas. This meant that the planet's temperature cooled, causing **deserts to shrink, and lush forests to grow**. These changes created a lot more food for wildlife. As a result, the Jurassic period saw many **new species** of dinosaur appear.

## COLOUR
THE DINOSAURS IN.

It was during the Jurassic period that the stout Stegosaurus (STEG-oh-SORE-uss), the fierce Allosaurus (al-oh-SORE-us), and the super-sized Brachiosaurus (brackee-oh-SORE-uss) existed.

# The Cretaceous period

The longest period of the Mesozoic Era was the Cretaceous, which spanned from 145–65 million years ago. It was a time of **incredible diversity**, when many new species of dinosaurs appeared. One reason for this was that the continents that formed when Pangaea split drifted farther apart, **spreading dinosaurs to new corners of the Earth.** At the time, the continents were still different to the way they are today, but they started to look more like they do now.

PRESENT DAY

North America
Europe
Asia
Africa
South America
Australia
Antarctica

## COLOUR
THE CONTINENTS AND TRY TO MATCH EACH MODERN VERSION.

Triceratops

**DRAW** MORE DINOSAURS ON THE MAP.

The Cretaceous period was when some of the most well known dinosaurs existed, including Tyrannosaurus rex, Triceratops, and Velociraptor.

Earth's continents are still moving today, just very slowly!

Tyrannosaurus rex

The biggest dinosaurs of all, sauropods, only ate plants. They had to graze **all day** to get enough fuel. It's amazing there was enough to go around!

# Herbivores

The word dinosaur means "terrible lizard", but that doesn't mean they were all terrible! It's true many dinosaurs were predators, but most were actually **plant-eaters** (herbivores). By the time the Jurassic period rolled around, the Earth was covered with forests – or to a herbivore, **free dinner** for the taking! They just had to get there before all the other dinosaurs showed up!

**DRAW** MORE DINOSAURS GETTING THEIR DINNER

CYCADS

BABY GINGKOS

FERNS

**DRAW** FOOD IN THE DINOSAUR'S BASKETS BEFORE IT'S ALL GONE!

# Carnivores

While the majority of dinosaurs happily munched on plants, carnivores (meat-eaters) survived by eating lizards, insects, and other dinosaurs. Although many carnivores had similar dining habits, they were often very different. For example, Compsognathus **(COMP-sog-NAITH-us)**, was only the size of a chicken, and scavenged a lot of its meals, but the monstrous Carnotaurus **(CAR-no-TAWR-us)** was about twice as big as a man. Imagine how much it would need to eat to get full up!

**DRAW** A MEAL FOR THE HUNGRY CARNOTAURUS.

Smaller carnivores sometimes had to **scavenge** for their meat.

Carnivores had large hearts and lungs which helped them get lots of oxygen. This made it easier for them to hunt! Remember, their dinner could run away from them!

SAVE THE TENONTOSAURUS. **DRAW** A SAFE ROUTE OUT OF THE FOREST.

**START**

# Pack attack

Not all predators were big, and sometimes they were **smaller than their prey**. (Imagine your dinner being bigger than you!) To turn the tables, dinosaurs such as Deinonychus **(dye-NON-ee-cuss)** would hunt prey that had been separated from its **herd**, and gang up before moving in for the kill.

FINISH

Deinonychus and
Velociraptor were among
the deadliest pack hunters.

**COLOUR** THE FOREST AND CAMOUFLAGE THE SCUTELLOSAURUS.

# Habitats

The world the dinosaurs lived in was very different to ours. Dinosaurs lived in all sorts of **environments**, and were always looking for the right place to call **home**.

COLOUR THE DESERT.

**Deserts** – the Earth's climate was **warmer** than it is today, and large areas of desert were found throughout the Mesozoic era.

DRAW MORE DINOSAURS OCCUPYING THE SCRUBLAND.

**Scrubland** – This **semi-desert** supported plants that didn't require much water to survive, and was home for many early species of dinosaur.

Too steep!

FINISH THE REST OF THE MOUNTAIN RANGE.

**Mountains** – These appeared at a growing rate as the Earth's **plates shifted** over the years, but it's likely there wasn't a great deal of food there.

**COLOUR** THE CROC.

**Swampland** – Swamps were very common throughout the Cretaceous, and were home to **hadrosaurs** and many other herbivores.

Too wet!

**FINISH** THE RIVER.

**Riverbanks** – All living things need water to survive, so a lot of dinosaurs settled close to **riverbanks** and **coasts**.

FINISH THE FOREST AND **DRAW** ANOTHER TRICERATOPS.

**Forests** – Even though dense forests would have helped predators to blend in, they were a **rich source of food** for herbivores such as Triceratops **(try-SERRA-tops)**.

# Therizinosaurus

**ROLL UP ROLL UP**

Small head

Lethal claws

Feathers

Potbelly

Stumpy feet

It's easy to see why Therizinosaurus was nicknamed **"scythe lizard"**. Its monstrous claws were almost 1m (3ft) long.

The strangest dinosaur had to be Therizinosaurus (**THERRY-zin-oh-SORE-us**). When scientists studied the fossils, they couldn't believe how unusual it was. They stood on their back legs like most predators, but they only ate plants. They had lethal claws, but didn't use them for hunting. They had small heads, feathers, stumpy feet, and their large digestive systems meant they had big **potbellies**! How weird!

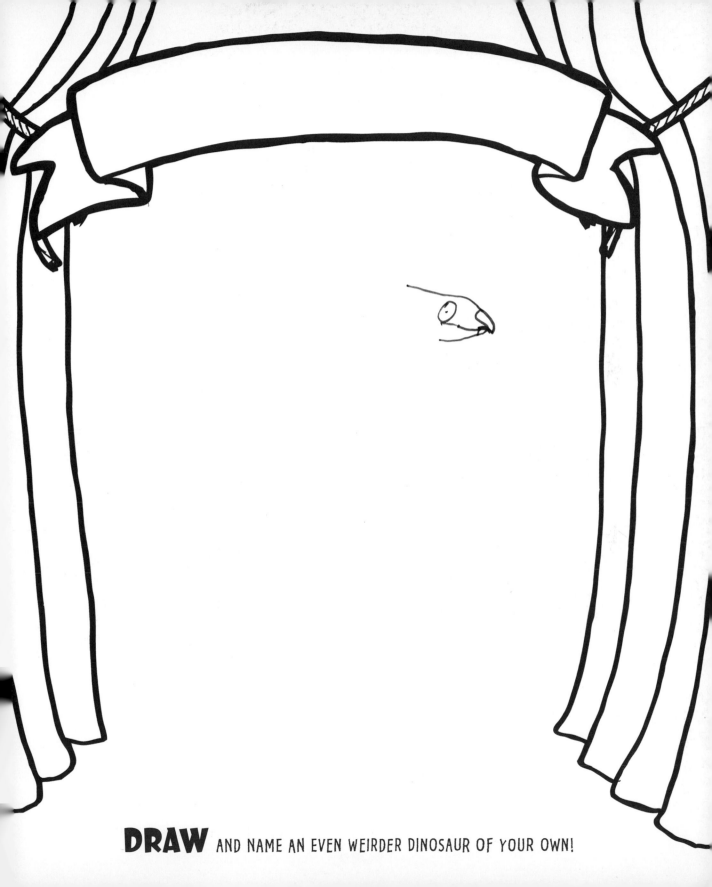

**DRAW** AND NAME AN EVEN WEIRDER DINOSAUR OF YOUR OWN!

# Crests and plumes

Many dinosaurs had impressive crests and plumes on their heads to **attract mates** and to **threaten rivals**. They came in all shapes and sizes. Can you imagine what they might look like?

PARASAUROLOPHUS

Guanlong **(GWON-long)**, an early relative of Tyrannosaurus rex, was discovered in China in 2006.

GUANLONG

CRYOLOPHOSAURUS

**DRAW** CRESTS AND PLUMES ON THE DINOSAURS, THEN MAKE UP YOUR OWN AND GIVE THEM NAMES.

# Sticking together

If you were a herbivore, danger could be lurking around every corner. Plant-eaters such as Tenontosaurus **(ten-NON-toe-SORE-us)** that weren't able to defend themselves, looked for **safety in numbers** and travelled in herds to make sneaky predators think twice about attacking them.

Modern animals such as zebras and wildebeests travel in herds for the same reason.

**FINISH** AND **COLOUR** THE REST OF THE HERD.

# Bone dome

Pachycephalosaurus (PACK-ee-sef-ah-low-SORE-us) was famous for a very unusual feature. They had a huge, thick skull shaped a little like a **bowling ball**, which might look ugly, but don't tell them that! Experts believe they used it like a **battering ram** to discourage predators and to intimidate rivals, similar to how stags butt heads today. However, it's also possible that it was just for show.

The dome was made of **solid bone**, and was 25cm (10in) thick!

The word pachycephalosaur means "thick-headed lizard".

# Walking weapons

Danger was everywhere during the time of the dinosaurs – even predators were sometimes **prey for bigger dinosaurs themselves!** Only the biggest and strongest such as Tyrannosaurus rex could feel safe at all times. The scariest predators didn't need any special weapons to take down their prey – they had their own!

T. rex's jaw was so powerful that it could **crush the bones** of its prey with ease.

**Allosaurus** had a weak jaw, but very sharp teeth. It's possible it **slashed** its prey rather than try to bite it.

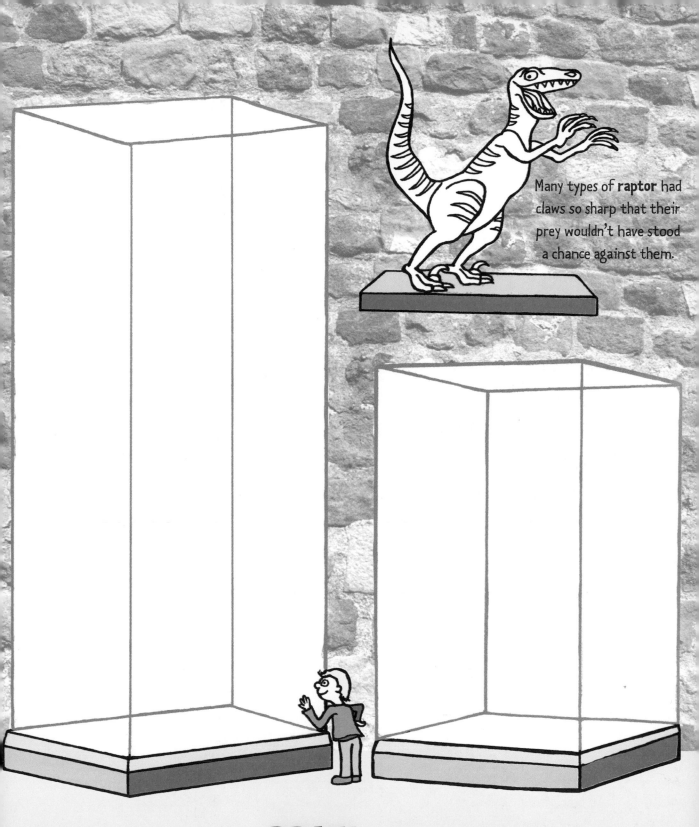

Many types of **raptor** had claws so sharp that their prey wouldn't have stood a chance against them.

**DRAW** YOUR OWN DINOSAURS WITH DEADLY WEAPONS.

# Defence

No dinosaur wanted to be an easy meal. Some would try to fight off predators with their claws and teeth, but others – such as a group of dinosaurs called **ankylosaurs** – had special defensive features such as plates and spines. One of which was Euoplocephalus **(YOU-owe-plo-SEFF-ah-luss)**, which was **built like a tank**, and had a crushing club made of bone at the end of its tail, that it would swing at attacking predators.

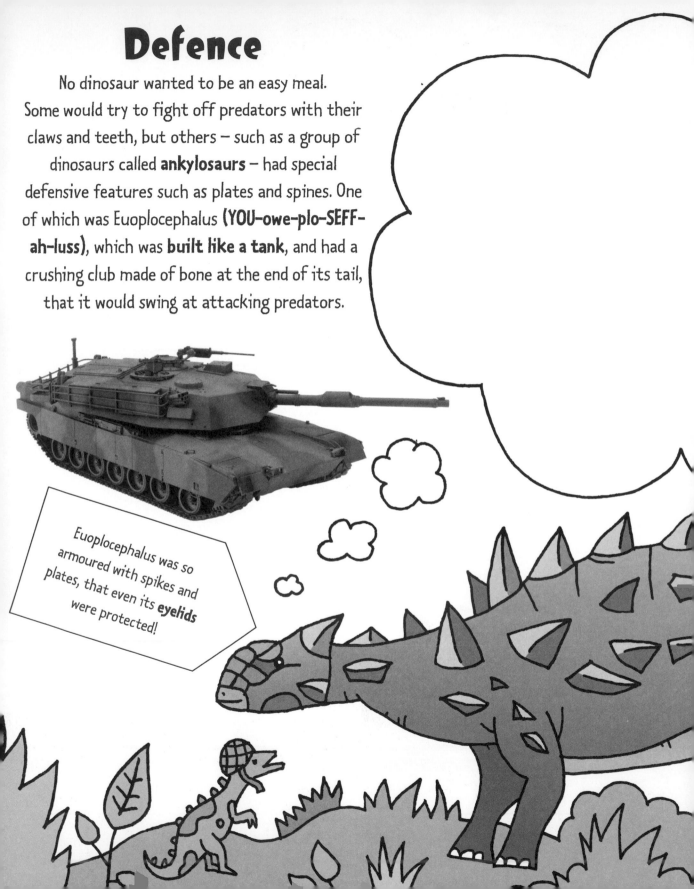

Euoplocephalus was so armoured with spikes and plates, that even its **eyelids** were protected!

# DESIGN YOUR OWN ARMOURED DINOSAUR.

# FIGHTING BACK

When under attack from predators, dinosaurs were faced with a choice: to either **run or fight**. And sometimes the best defence was a good offence. Several herbivores had more than just armour, and were equipped with deadly weapons of their own to help them **fight back** against their enemies.

## STEGOSAURUS

Stegosaurus had **razor sharp** spikes on its tail, which it could whip at enemies.

## PENTACERATOPS

Pentaceratops and other ceratopsians could use their large **horns** as weapons of defence.

## IGUANODON

Iguanodon had sharp **spikes** on its hands to jab at attackers.

## DIPLODOCUS

Aside from being huge, Diplodocus could use its long tail like a **whip**.

**DRAW** THE FIGHTING DINOSAURS.

**FINISH**
DRAWING THE
SPINES ON
THE DINOSAURS.

OURANOSAURUS

# Spines and sails

It wasn't just their teeth and claws that helped dinosaurs stand out. Several dinosaurs had sail-like spines on their backs and necks. While these would have mainly been used to **attract mates** and **scare off rivals**, experts believe that they might also have helped dinosaurs manage their body temperature.

RAYOSOSAURUS

SPINOSAURUS

One of the most impressive spines belonged to **Spinosaurus**, the largest predator to ever walk the Earth. It was **even bigger** than Tyrannosaurus rex!

# Mini monster

Who says you had to be big to be a predator? Compsognathus **(COMP-sog-NAITH-us)**, a predator from the Jurassic period, was no bigger than a **chicken!** It used its speed and agility to chase down fast-moving lizards and insects, scavenge other predators' kills, and even sometimes **gang up** and take on larger prey.

It may be small, but it was fast. Despite its size, Compsognathus could **run at speeds of more than 40kph** (25mph).

40

# DRAW

THE REST OF THE
COMPSOGNATHUS PACK.

Compsognathus may have
been covered in **feathers,
fuzz,** or **scales** to help
it keep warm.

# Grazing giants

The Jurassic saw the rise of the sauropods – the largest creatures to ever walk the Earth. The largest of these, Argentinosaurus **(ARE-jen-teen-oh-SORE-us)**, grew to up to 36m (118ft) long, and weighed as much as **13 elephants**. It would have needed to eat all day to have the energy to move!

A single Brachiosaurus would need to eat around 180kg of food **every day!**

**COLOUR** THE ARGENTINOSAURUS GREEN.

# COLOUR

THE DIPLODOCUS RED.

Sauropods had long necks so they reach food other dinosaurs couldn't. Some could even stand up on their **hind legs**!

Sauropods were plant-eaters, but that doesn't mean they couldn't defend themselves from predators. They were so massive that they could **crush** any attackers.

## COLOUR THE
BRACHIOSAURUS YELLOW.

## COLOUR THE
SALTASAURUS BLUE.

# Titans of the Earth

Tyrannosaurus rex gets all the glory, but there were plenty of other giant predators around. In fact, T. rex's "cousin" Giganotosaurus (gig-AN-oh-toe-SORE-rus) was just as big. It's lucky they lived 10 million years apart, or there would have been **nasty fights** over their dinner!

Experts believe that Giganotosaurus had a brain the shape of a **banana**!

No complete Giganotosaurus skeleton has ever been found, but experts believe they were about 13.5m (45ft) long, and would have weighed as much as **125 people**!

**COLOUR** THE CARNOTAURUS RED.

**COLOUR** THE GIGANOTOSAURUS BLUE.

**COLOUR** THE TYRANNOSAURUS GREEN.

**COLOUR** THE TYRANNOTITANS YELLOW.

**COLOUR** THE CARCHARODONTOSAURUS PURPLE.

DRAW MORE PARVICURSORS.

Brachiosaurus may have been big, but there wasn't a lot going on upstairs — its brain was only about the size of a **grapefruit**!

# Little and large

Dinosaurs came in all shapes and sizes, and while we usually think of them as colossal **giants** roaming the land, a few of them were actually **tiny**. For example, while the gigantic Brachiosaurus (**brack-ee-oh-SORE-us**), a sauropod from the Jurassic, grew to up to 25m (82ft) long from head to tail, the tiny Parvicursor (**PAR-vee-cur-SORE**), from the Late Cretaceous, only grew to about 45cm (18in)!

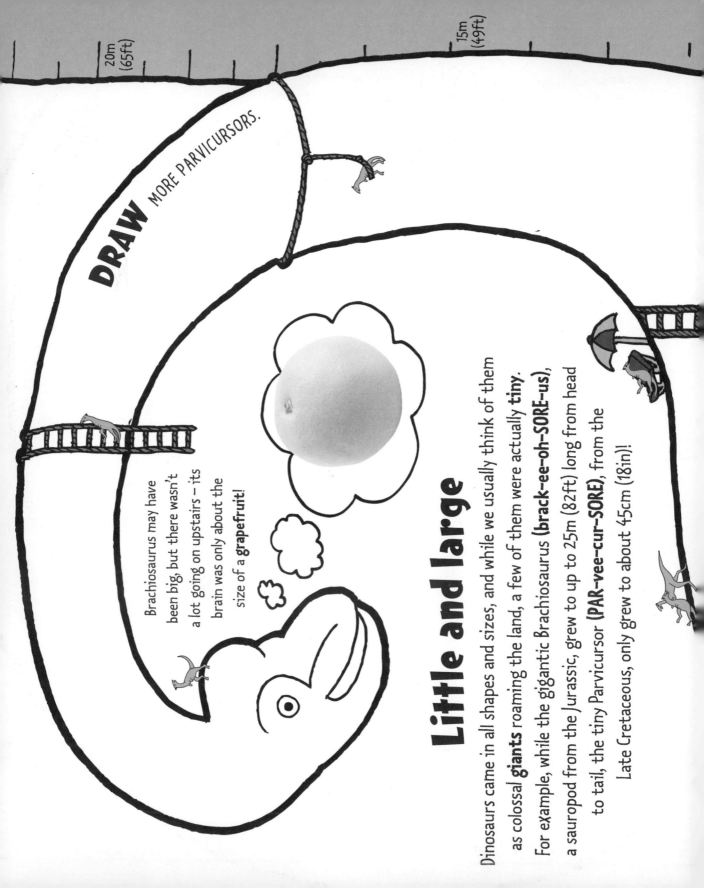

Parvicursors had a fairly large claw on each hand, but they were probably for **digging** rather than defending themselves.

# Fast and slow

Fossils give us clues about how fast dinosaurs could run. It varied between species, and while no dinosaur was as fast as the fastest modern land animal, the **cheetah**, which can run at **114kph** (70mph), smaller dinosaurs could probably reach very fast speeds. Others, such as the giant sauropods were very slow.

Brachiosaurus weighed so much that it probably couldn't move faster than 6kph (3.5mph)!

Ankylosaurus was built like a tank, so it **didn't need to** run away from predators, so it was probably slow-moving.

Ankylosaurus

Brachiosaurus

**DRAW** MORE RACING DINOSAURS.

Predators walked on two legs to be able to move fast enough to catch their food.

# Predator and prey

In order to survive, all dinosaurs had to eat, and while herbivores were happy to chomp on plants, carnivores had something a little fresher in mind! Because of this, plant-eaters had to always be on the lookout for **hungry predators** ready to turn them into their next meal!

CAN YOU TELL THE HUNTERS FROM THE HUNTED?
**COLOUR** THE PREDATORS ORANGE, AND THE PREY YELLOW.

Herbivores were slow-moving, and walked on four legs.

# Stegosaurus

Don't let the fact that Stegosaurus **(STEG-oh-SORE-uss)** was a plant-eater trick you into thinking it was easy prey. It grew to up to 9m (30ft) long, and weighed **4 tonnes.** And with its impressive plates and **sharp spiky tail**, it was well equipped with the tools to fend off even the most fierce predators of the Jurassic period.

**FINISH** THE SPIKES ON THE TAIL.

Stegosaurus certainly wasn't the smartest dinosaur in the herd. Its brain was no bigger than a **walnut!**

Certain dinosaurs would **sit on their nests** the way that birds do.

**START**

# Baby dinosaurs

Dinosaurs were reptiles, so scientists always thought that they probably laid eggs. But it wasn't until 1920, when the remains of the eggs and nests of a dinosaur called Oviraptor **(oh-vee-RAP-tor)** were found in the **Gobi Desert, China** that they could say for sure. This huge discovery helped scientists to understand much more about dinosaur life.

The temperature of dinosaur eggs could **determine the gender** of the babies. The warmer the eggs were, the more likely it was that they would hatch as males.

**DRAW** THE OVIRAPTOR A SAFE ROUTE BACK TO HER NEST.

FINISH

Oviraptor would sometimes dig its nests from sand or earth.

# Parasaurolophus

During the Cretaceous, a group of dinosaurs called hadrosaurs, or "duck-billed" dinosaurs emerged. Among these was Parasaurolophus **(PA-ra-SORE-oh-LOAF-uss)** – a large plant-eater with hundreds of grinding teeth for mashing up food. They were common, and travelled in large herds, and are sometimes thought of as the dinosaur version of cows!

Unlike most other herbivores, hadrosaurs could walk on either two or four legs.

Parasaurolophus was **surprisingly big** for prey, and adults could grow to be 10m (33ft) long. No wonder it was a favourite meal for many carnivores – it made for very big portions!

# CONNECT THE DOTS TO REVEAL THE PICTURE.

Nobody is certain if dinosaurs **communicated with sound**, but experts believe they probably did. One reason for this is that Parasaurolophus' crest contained a series of tubes that **connected to the nostrils** – which meant it might work like a trumpet.

# Deinonychus

While teeth were the weapon of choice for many dinosaurs, others dealt damage with their **claws**. Perhaps the scariest of these dinosaurs was Deinonychus **(dye-NON-ee-cuss)**, a speedy pack hunter from the Early Cretaceous. As well as the sharp claws on its hands, Deinonychus had a monstrous upturned **sickle claw** on each foot that it used to deliver lethal strikes.

Deinonychus means "terrible claw" and it's easy to see why!

Deinonychus was lethal, but it was only 3m (10ft) long, so it roamed in packs to take down larger prey.

**FINISH** THE REST OF THE DEINONYCHUS PACK.

The long tail was held stiff to help with balance while running.

# Dressed to frill

Known for their **horns** and neck frills, ceratopsians were a group of herbivores from the Cretaceous period. They might look scary, but their large frills and horns were **only for protection**, and their sharp beaks were used to **rip up plants** for food.

Although they look a little like them, ceratopsians have no link to the modern **rhinoceros**.

**COLOUR** THE PROTOCERATOPS GREEN.

There is a lot of fossil evidence to suggest that there were many **fierce battles** between Triceratops and T. rex.

**COLOUR** STYRACOSAURUS PURPLE.

**COLOUR** THE PENTACERATOPS BLUE.

Pentaceratops had a **giant skull** measuring 3m (10ft) long!

**COLOUR** THE TRICERATOPS RED.

**COLOUR** THE CHASMOSAURUS YELLOW.

# The ultimate predator

Tyrannosaurus rex (**TIE-ran-oh-SORE-us**), or T. rex for short, was a ferocious hunter with a massive skull and **bone-crushing teeth**. At 4m (13ft) tall and 12m (40ft) long, it weighed as much as **five cars**. It was one of the biggest predators that ever lived, and terrorized the forests of what is now North America until it became extinct 65 million years ago. Phew!

**FINISH** THE T. REX'S DINNER INSIDE ITS STOMACH.

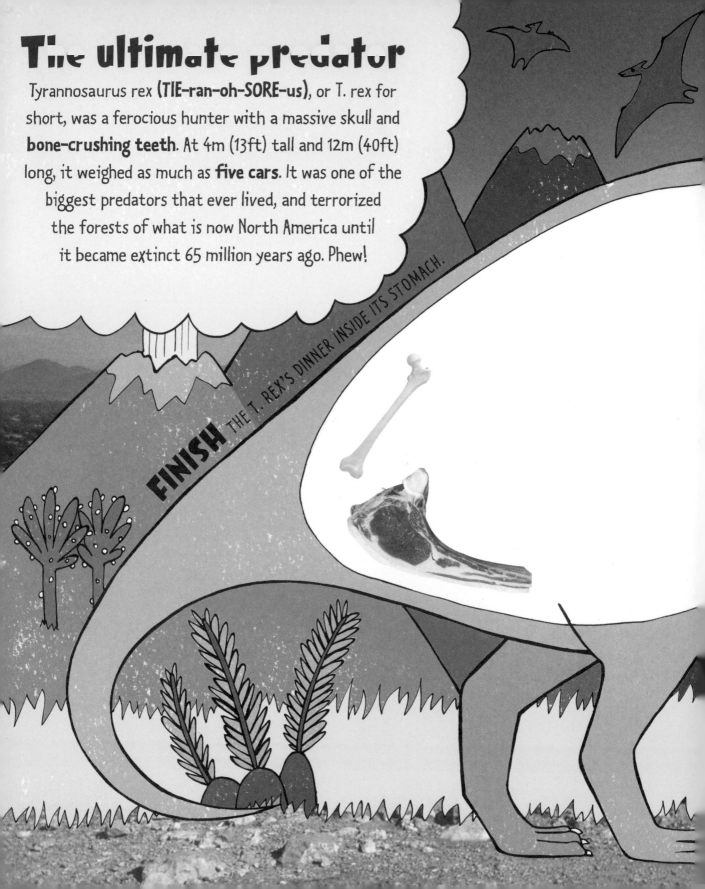

Tyrannosaurus means "tyrant lizard" in Greek.

I am the king of the dinosaurs, and I had very **bad breath**! Some experts believe that rotting meat stuck in my teeth could have made my bite **poisonous**, as well as crushing.

**DRAW** ANOTHER T. REX IN THE BACKGROUND.

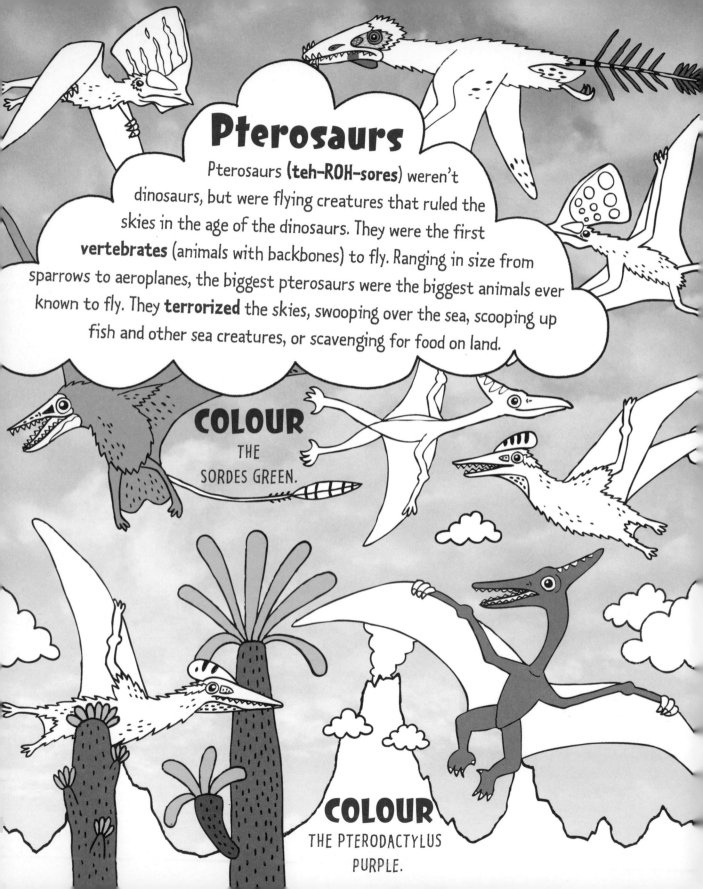

# Pterosaurs

Pterosaurs (**teh-ROH-sores**) weren't dinosaurs, but were flying creatures that ruled the skies in the age of the dinosaurs. They were the first **vertebrates** (animals with backbones) to fly. Ranging in size from sparrows to aeroplanes, the biggest pterosaurs were the biggest animals ever known to fly. They **terrorized** the skies, swooping over the sea, scooping up fish and other sea creatures, or scavenging for food on land.

**COLOUR** THE SORDES GREEN.

**COLOUR** THE PTERODACTYLUS PURPLE.

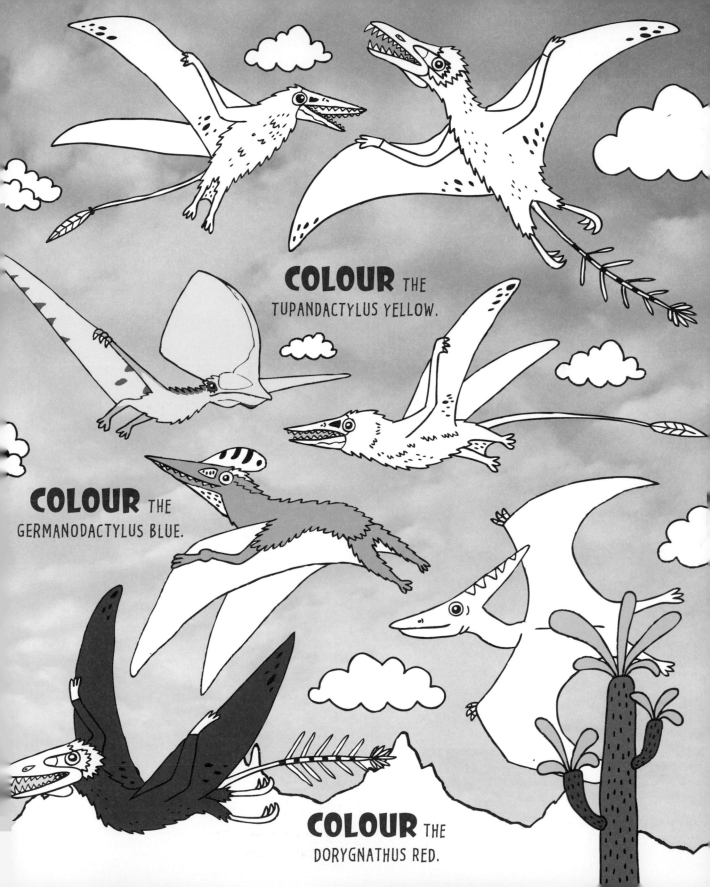

**COLOUR** THE TUPANDACTYLUS YELLOW.

**COLOUR** THE GERMANODACTYLUS BLUE.

**COLOUR** THE DORYGNATHUS RED.

Quetzalcoatlus were **soarers** rather than fliers, and relied on strong winds to travel through the air.

**DRAW** MORE SOARING QUETZALCOATLUS.

# Quetzalcoatlus

The largest creature ever to fly was the monstrous pterosaur Quetzalcoatlus **(KWETS-ul-coe-AT-luss)**. This giant ruled the Cretaceous skies, casting a giant shadow over the Earth wherever it flew. Its **wingspan** was a massive 12m (39ft) across, the size of a small plane!

# The first bird

Believe it or not, birds are the descendants of dinosaurs. Technically, **they are** dinosaurs — the only surviving group! The earliest known bird is Archaeopteryx **(ar-kee-OP-ter-ix)**, which appeared in the Jurassic period. It had the feathered tail and wings of a bird, but the claws of a dinosaur.

## COLOUR
IN THE FUNKY FEATHERS.

Archaeopteryx was about the same size as a modern raven.

Nobody knows
what colour their
feathers were.
For all we know
they could be
**bright pink
or orange!**

**COLOUR** THE TYLOSAURUS PURPLE.

**COLOUR** THE PLESIOSAURUS BLUE.

# Creatures of the deep

Dinosaurs ruled the land, and pterosaurs dominated the sky, but it was **marine reptiles** that **lurked beneath the waves** during the Mesozoic Era. The largest of these massive monsters could grow up to 20m (70ft) long, and while they spent their lives in the water, they all **breathed air**.

The skull of Deinosuchus (**die-no-SUE-kus**) – a relative of modern crocodiles was 1.8m (6ft) long, and a fully grown Deinosuchus weighed up to 5 tonnes!

**COLOUR** THE DEINOSUCHUS YELLOW.

**COLOUR** THE ELASMOSAURUS RED.

Elasmosaurus had **72 bones** in its neck!

**COLOUR** THE KRONOSAURUS GREEN.

# Rhomaleosaurus

The words "sea monsters" come to mind when you think of Rhomaleosaurus **(ROME-alley-oh-SORE-us).** They grew to up to 7m (21ft) long, and in many ways, were like the aquatic version of Tyrannosaurus rex. They **terrorized** the Jurassic seas, feasting on fish, squid, and smaller marine reptiles.

Rhomaleosaurus glided through the water using its four flippers like wings to **"fly"** underwater. Penguins and sea lions do a similar thing today.

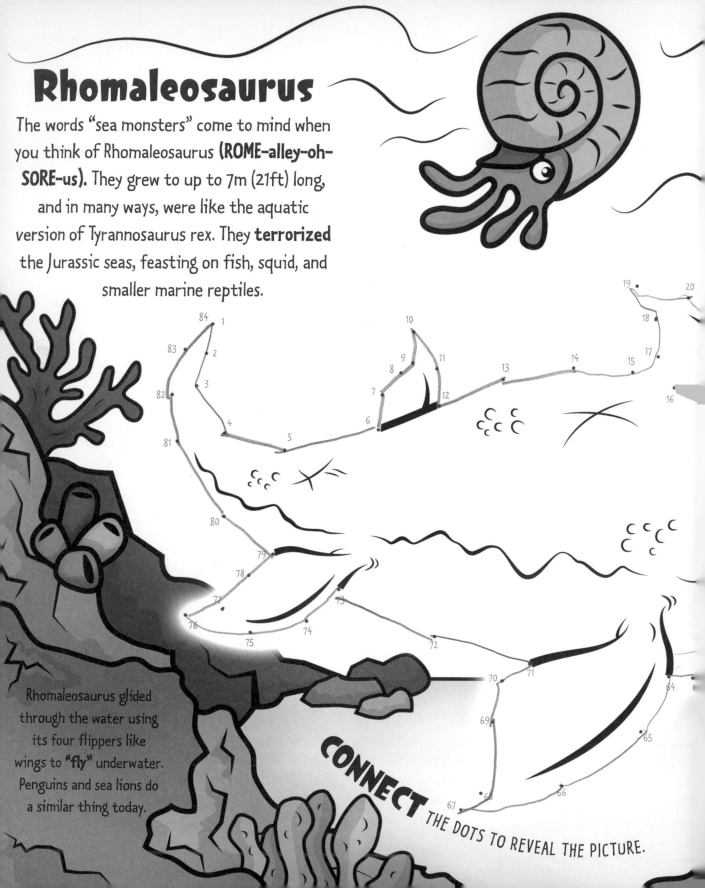

CONNECT THE DOTS TO REVEAL THE PICTURE.

It's thought that like a lot of ocean predators, Rhomaleosaurus had a pale belly and dark back, making it **harder to spot** from both above and below.

# Megatooth

If you thought plesiosaurs were scary, you're in for a shock. Megatooth (**MEG-a-tooth**), an ancestor of the great white shark, may have existed 40 million years after the time of the dinosaurs, pterosaurs, and marine reptiles, but it was the all-time **ultimate monster of the deep**. It grew to up to 20m (67ft) long, weighed up to 100 tonnes, and is probably the most ferocious predator ever.

**START**

Megatooth's teeth were the size of dinner plates, and they had about **250** of them. That would take a lot of toothpaste to clean!

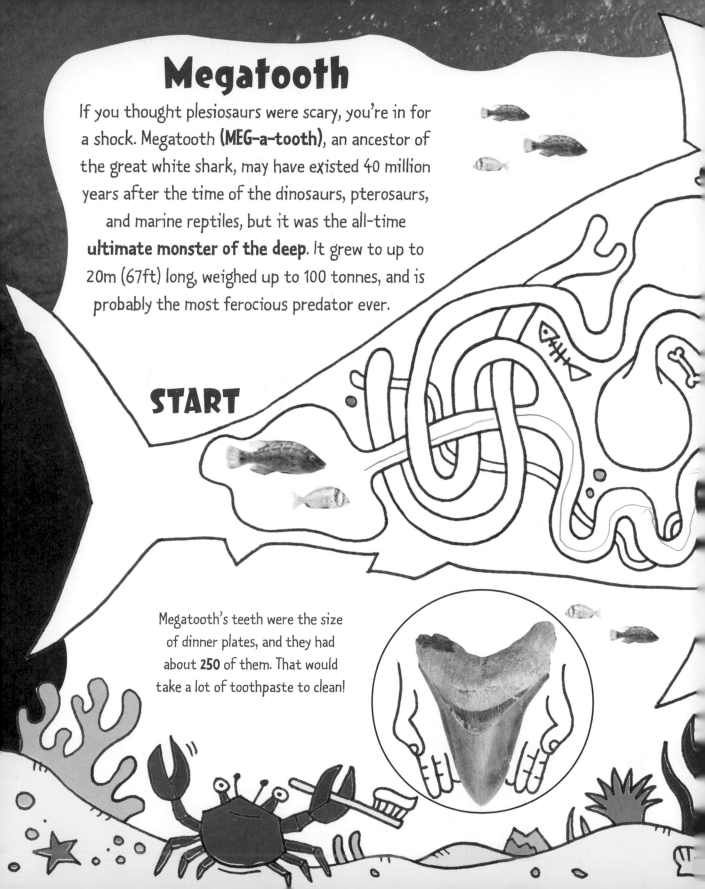

Ahh! I'm getting out of here!!

FINISH

DRAW A WAY OUT OF THE MEGATOOTH MAZE.

Great white shark

# The ultimate beast!

All dinosaurs were amazing creatures, but some dinosaurs were a little more spectacular than others. These dinosaurs were among the **fastest, strongest, scariest, and most interesting** to have lived – but can you imagine what a dinosaur with all of these qualities combined would be like?

## LONGEST NECK
### MAMENCHISAURUS

| PERIOD | JURASSIC |
|---|---|
| SIZE | ★★★★★ |
| SPEED | ★ |
| INTELLIGENCE | ★★ |

## BIGGEST BRAIN
### TROODON

| PERIOD | CRETACEOUS |
|---|---|
| SIZE | ★ |
| SPEED | ★★★★ |
| INTELLIGENCE | ★★★★★ |

## STRONGEST BITE
### T. REX

| PERIOD | CRETACEOUS |
|---|---|
| SIZE | ★★★★ |
| SPEED | ★★★ |
| INTELLIGENCE | ★ |

# DRAW THE SCARIEST DINOSAURS THAT NEVER LIVED BY COMBINING THE FEATURES OF THE OTHER DINOSAURS.

## BEST ARMOUR
### ANKYLOSAURUS

| PERIOD | CRETACEOUS |
|---|---|
| SIZE | ★★★ |
| SPEED | ★★ |
| INTELLIGENCE | ★★ |

## DEADLIEST CLAWS
### UTAHRAPTOR

| PERIOD | CRETACEOUS |
|---|---|
| SIZE | ★★★ |
| SPEED |  |
| INTELLIGENCE |  |

## FASTEST LEGS
### STRUTHIOMIMUS

| PERIOD | CRETACEOUS |
|---|---|
| SIZE | ★★ |
| SPEED |  |
| INTELLIGENCE |  |

# Where did they go?

At the end of the Cretaceous period, dinosaurs were **thriving** like never before. Then, about 65 million years ago – with the exception of several species of bird – they **mysteriously died out**. The reason why this happened puzzled scientists for years, but they now believe that a **massive meteorite** crashed into the Earth. This caused earthquakes, tsunamis, volcanic eruptions, and threw up a cloud of dust so big that it blocked out the Sun.

In Mexico there is the **remains of a crater** 180km (112 miles) wide. Experts believe this is where the meteorite crash landed.

EEEK

**DRAW** MORE SCARED DINOSAURS!

Other theories about why the dinosaurs became extinct include an ice age, and a dinosaur **plague**.

Scientists estimate that the meteorite would have been roughly 10km (6 miles) wide, and struck the Earth at a **staggering** 100,000kph (62,000mph!)

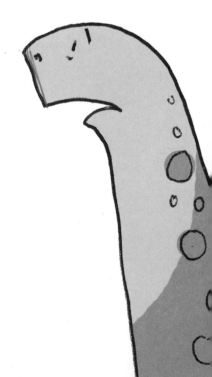

# THE DAILY DINO

# WHAT SURVIVED?

**SEE THE LATEST IN DINOSAUR FASHION!**

In the millions of years that followed the destruction of the dinosaurs, many new species of animal **came and went**. However, a handful of creatures, other than birds from the Mesozoic Era, managed to **survive the extinction** and are still around today – on land, in the sea, and in the air.

**DRAW** THE REST OF THE SURVIVORS.

Various species of **fish, shark, and jellyfish** were among the creatures that survived in the seas.

was only **small animals** such as lizards, insects, snakes, and crocodiles that survived on land.

hile a lot of **early birds** became extinct, a few species managed to survive, and so did many flying insects.

**FINISH**

A MODERN
CITY WITH
PEOPLE AND
DINOSAURS
LIVING
TOGETHER!

# What if they weren't extinct?

In the years that followed the extinction caused by the meteorite, the world became a **very different** place. The continents shifted, the climate changed, and thousands of new species of animal and plant evolved. Eventually, human beings emerged and became the Earth's most **dominant species.** But can you imagine what the world would be like if the dinosaurs hadn't become extinct? Would we keep dinosaurs as pets? Or would they be destructive and try to eat us?

# Turning to stone

Everything we know about dinosaurs, pterosaurs, and marine reptiles, we learned from their **fossilized remains**. Fossils are the stone remnants of things that lived long ago that have been preserved in the Earth's layers.

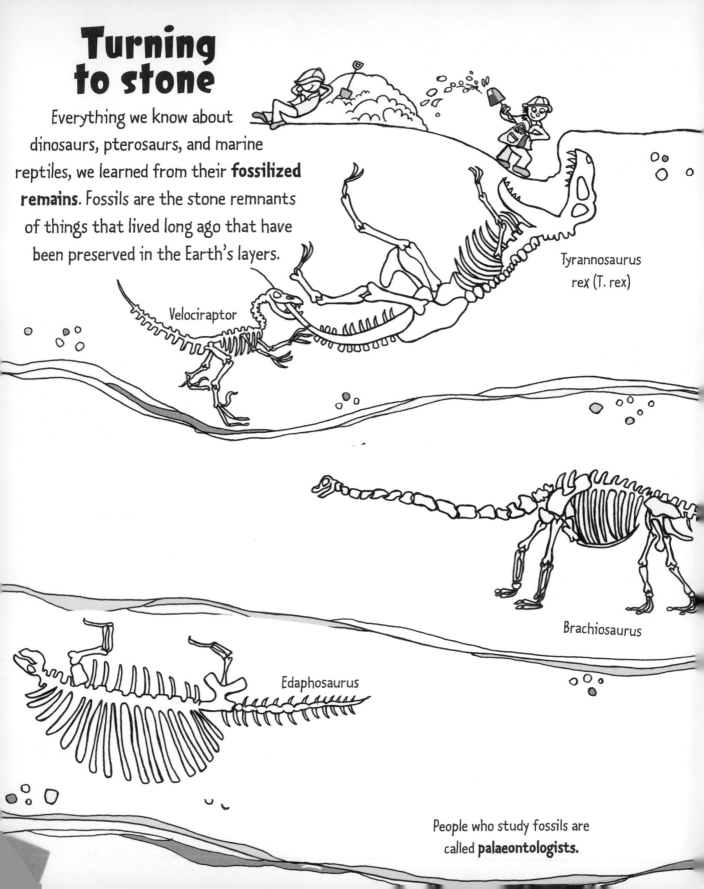

Tyrannosaurus rex (T. rex)

Velociraptor

Brachiosaurus

Edaphosaurus

People who study fossils are called **palaeontologists**.

Fossils are rare. Most dinosaurs simply decayed and **disappeared forever**. Only a few of the dinosaurs that lived have been, or will be, found as fossils.

Triceratops

Pterodactylus

**DRAW** MORE FOSSILS IN THE EARTH.

Fossilized eggs, feathers, footprints, and even **dinosaur poo** have been found. These all help us to understand more about prehistoric life.

# Studying fossils

Not only are fossils **rare**, but they're also very fragile, and it takes a lot of hard work and patience for **palaeontologists** (fossil experts) to get them out of the ground. When a fossil is discovered, huge dig sites are set up, and it can take months before the fossils are fully excavated for study in a lab.

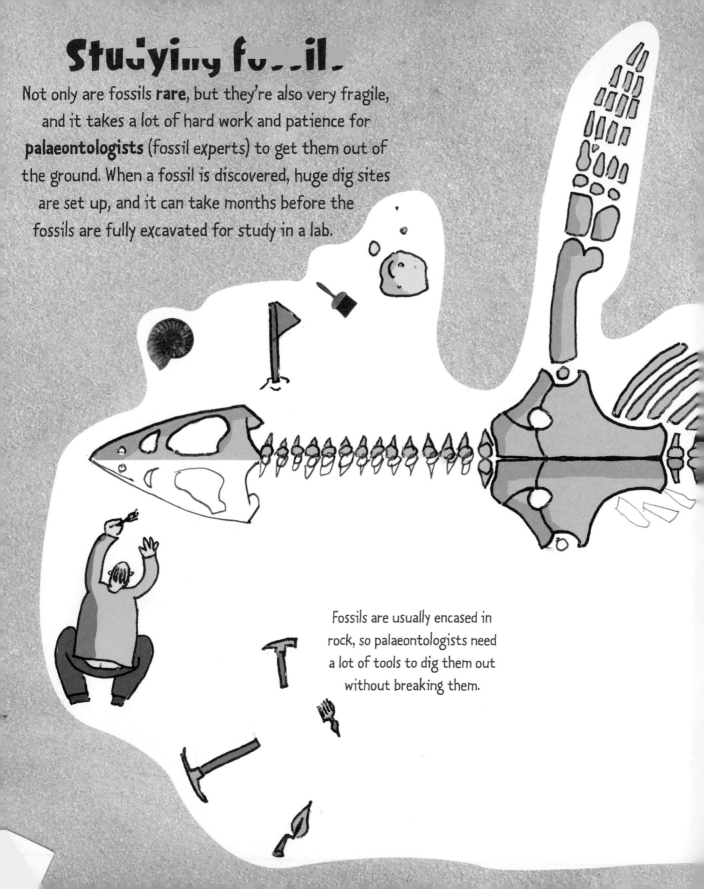

Fossils are usually encased in rock, so palaeontologists need a lot of tools to dig them out without breaking them.

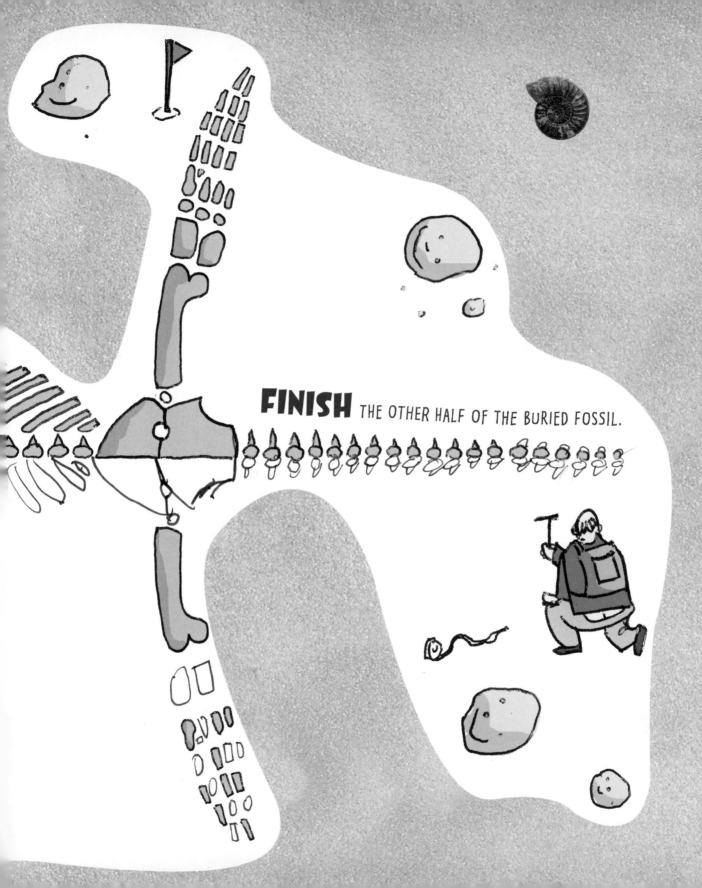

**FINISH** THE OTHER HALF OF THE BURIED FOSSIL.

# Dinosaurs on display

The dinosaurs might not be around anymore, but that shouldn't stop you from seeing what they were like. Museums have incredible dinosaur exhibits on display, including fossils that are **hundreds of millions** of years old, and even full skeletons!

SOME OF THE T. REX BONES HAVE FALLEN OFF! **DRAW** THEM BACK ON TO FINISH THE DISPLAY.

"Sue" the T. rex fossil at the Field Museum, Chicago, USA is the most complete T-Rex fossil in the world. It cost the museum a whopping **£5.2 million ($8.4 million)** when they bought it in 1997.

TYRANNOSAURUS REX

# Draw your own dinosaur

Now that you've learned all about these amazing creatures, draw **one of your own**. Who knows, one day a palaeontologist might discover one that looks just like it!

DESIGN, COLOUR AND NAME YOUR OWN DINOSAUR.

**DRAW** SOMETHING
**FANTASTIC**
TO FINISH THE SECTION.

TURN THE PAGE FOR...

# DOODLEPEDIA
## WOW

# DOODLEPEDIA
# WOW

# The race is on!

Motor racing is fast and exciting. The cars that compete in Formula 1 can reach speeds of up to 360 kph (225 mph)! To make the cars safe, controllable, and fast, the engineers use the science of **aerodynamics**. A Formula 1 car is designed so the air that travels over and past it doesn't slow the car down too much. A Formula 1 car travels fast enough to take off like an aeroplane, so it also uses the pressure of the **air** flowing over it to keep it firmly on the track. This **downforce** allows the tyres to grip the ground and gives the car more control.

The **downforce** created by a Formula 1 car at its top speed is **strong enough** for it to be **driven upside-down** along a roof of a tunnel.

**DESIGN** A WINNING, SUPER-FAST **RACING CAR!**

# Check your bags!

All luggage that is going on a plane has to be put through an airport **X-ray scanner**, which displays an image of what is inside each bag. The scanner operators are looking for **dangerous items**, such as weapons and other illegal things, but they must get to see some weird and wonderful things hidden in people's bags!

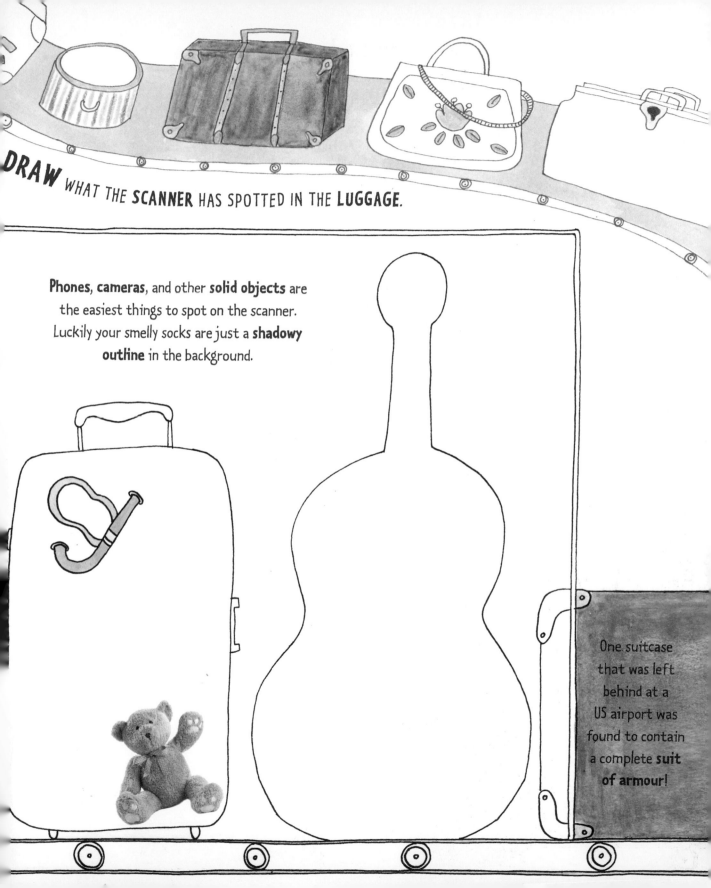

**DRAW** WHAT THE **SCANNER** HAS SPOTTED IN THE **LUGGAGE**.

Phones, cameras, and other solid objects are the easiest things to spot on the scanner. Luckily your smelly socks are just a shadowy outline in the background.

One suitcase that was left behind at a US airport was found to contain a complete suit of armour!

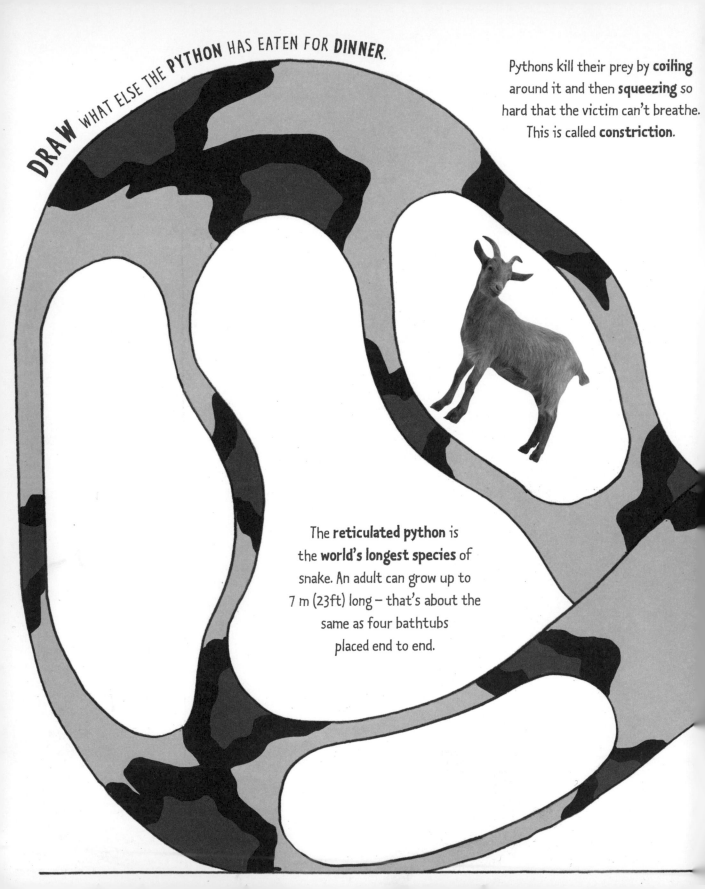

DRAW WHAT ELSE THE PYTHON HAS EATEN FOR DINNER.

Pythons kill their prey by **coiling** around it and then **squeezing** so hard that the victim can't breathe. This is called **constriction**.

The **reticulated python** is the **world's longest species** of snake. An adult can grow up to 7 m (23ft) long – that's about the same as four bathtubs placed end to end.

# Open wide!

Some large species of **python** really can eat a goat or a deer whole. But how does a snake swallow something that is bigger than its own mouth? The answer lies in its **jaws**, which are not hinged like ours but joined loosely by a **ligament**, like a piece of elastic. The ligament just keeps **stretching**, allowing the snake to open its jaws wider and wider until it has the whole prey in its mouth. Gulp!

# Surf's up!

**Surfing** is difficult and dangerous, but it's great fun! The trick is to hop onto the **surfboard** just before the wave **breaks** and then ride along the rolling wall of water. The best **surf waves** start miles out to sea. Storms creates **huge ripples** in the water that spread in all directions as waves. They may take days or even weeks to reach land. The waves break when they reach the beach because the shallow water makes the wave grow taller and taller – until it topples over.

**Big-wave surfing** involves waves more than 6 m (20 ft) high. Extreme surfers have ridden waves 21 m (70 ft) high – that's as tall as a seven-storey building!

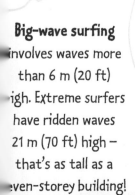

# Now wash your hands!

**Viruses** are a particular nasty type of germ. They are very, very small, in fact **millions** can fit on a pinhead only 2 mm (0.08 inch) wide! They can't survive for very long on their own, but once **inside the cells** of a living thing, such a plant, animal, or person, they can grow and **reproduce** very fast, making people feel very sick.

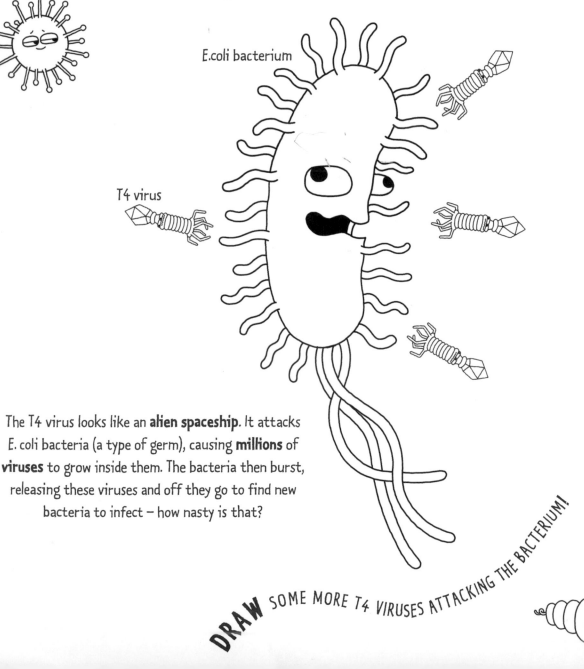

E.coli bacterium

T4 virus

The T4 virus looks like an **alien spaceship**. It attacks E. coli bacteria (a type of germ), causing **millions** of **viruses** to grow inside them. The bacteria then burst, releasing these viruses and off they go to find new bacteria to infect — how nasty is that?

DRAW SOME MORE T4 VIRUSES ATTACKING THE BACTERIUM!

# DRAW AND COLOUR SOME MORE VIRUSES.

Most **viruses** are between
5–300 nanometres (nm) long.
Considering that a nanometer is
**1,000,000,000th of a metre**,
that is pretty small!

The **Coup de Monde** is given to the winners of the **FIFA World Cup**.

FIFA WORLD CUP

This **spiral** trophy is given to the winner of the **Giro d'Italia** bicycle stage race.

Giro d'Italia

# It's a winner!

Nothing beats coming **first** in a sport and winning a **trophy**! In ancient times, winners at sporting events were often awarded a **silver goblet**. The tradition continues to this day, with **giant gold** and **silver trophies** given to **winning athletes and teams** in many major tournaments. To crown their moment of **glory**, winners may hold their trophy aloft and revel in the crowd's **cheers and applause**.

**DESIGN** SOME SHINY MEDALS.

# DESIGN YOUR OWN WINNER'S TROPHY.

**Medals** are awarded at the **Olympic Games** to **athletes** who finish first, second, or third in their event final.

# We need a hero!

HELP!!! The evil villain, cunningly disguised as a burglar, is making off with all the loot. Who can stop him? **Comic strips** like this one have been **entertaining** people since they were first published in 19th-century **newspapers**. Some of the most-loved characters are **superheroes**, such as Batman, Superman, and the Incredible Hulk.

Oh no! A dastardly robber has robbed a valuable painting...

HELP! WE NEED A SUPERHERO!

...but your superhero is here to help! Let's go get that cunning crook!

**DRAW** YOUR OWN SUPERHERO AND **FINISH** THE STORY.

"Hmm. Here's a clue that will lead me to the stolen painting..."

"...This is a great time to test out my new superhero gadget."

"Got you at last! Stop struggling, you scoundrel!" POW! CRASH! CRUNCH!

"It's off to the cells for you! Handcuff him!"

**THE END!**

**COLOUR** THE
CHEEKY SWINGING
MONKEYS.

**Baby** spider monkeys travel everywhere
by keeping a **tight grip** on their
mothers, especially when mum is
**hanging upside down.**

Spider monkeys don't have any **thumbs**, but still have a powerful grip.

# Hanging around!

**Spider monkeys** spend all day **hanging** around in the rainforests of South America. They are incredibly **agile**, swinging from branch to branch in search of their favourite foods, which include fruits, seeds, birds' eggs, and insects. They get their name from their **long, spidery arms and legs**. Their **tails** are longer than their bodies and they can use them like an extra limb. This allows them to use their hands and feet for feeding while keeping a **firm grip** on a branch using only their tails.

# Mask of art!

**African tribal masks** can look strange, scary, and fantastic. They have been a part of tribal life in Africa for thousands of years and are still used today in **dances, rituals, and ceremonies**. The **skill** of making the tribal masks is handed down from father to son and the **mask maker** is given a special role in the tribe. The masks are usually based on human faces, but aren't very realistic.

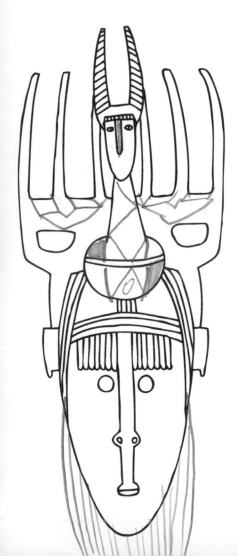

Some masks are **sacred** and are thought to possess **magical powers**.

Tribal mask makers used materials that were close to hand, like **wood, stone, and ivory** (animal tusks). The masks were painted using **local dyes** from **plants and soil**.

**DESIGN** YOUR OWN TRIBAL MASK.

# Down under in Australia!

When the first European **explorers** set out to map **Australia**, they had no idea what hideous **hazards** lay ahead. The middle part of the country, called the **outback**, turned out to be a vast, **desert-like plain**, with **baking temperatures**, and very **little water**. Many explorers died there from thirst, hunger, disease. The wildlife was not always friendly either – the outback contains some of the worlds' most **poisonous snakes** and **spiders**.

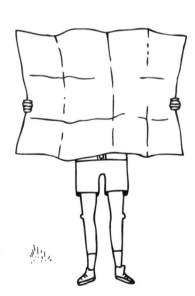

**DRAW** THE EXPLORERS' CAMPSITE AND **ADD** MORE HAIRY CAMELS AND SLITHERING SNAKES.

The explorer **Charles Sturt** thought there was an inland sea in the **outback** so he took a boat with him!

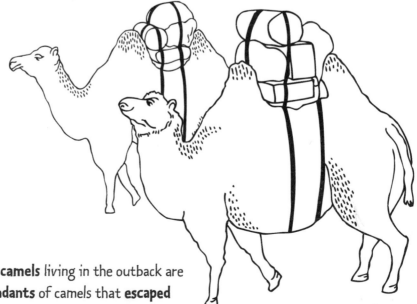

The **wild camels** living in the outback are **descendants** of camels that **escaped** from early explorations.

# Goal!

**Football** is the most popular sport on the planet, with an **incredible 3.5 billion fans worldwide** – that's more than half the world's population! The rules of the modern game were drawn up in Cambridge, England, in 1863, but football was **invented more than 2,000 years ago in China**. It caught on in England about 800 years ago, before being **banned for 300 years** after games got too violent. Today football is played in **every country** in the world.

DRAW MORE PLAYERS AND MAKE A WHOLE TEAM.

Whistles were introduced to football in 1878, but the **yellow and red cards** were not used until the 1970 World Cup in Mexico.

The **first ever World Cup** took place in Uruguay in 1930 with **80,000 people watching** the match.

# Blast off!

**Outer space** is only 100 km (60 miles) away, but it's uphill all the way! To get there you need the incredible power of a **rocket**. Built like gigantic fireworks, rockets are pushed upwards at high speed by the force of the exhaust fumes from burning fuel being pushed out of its nozzles. Rockets reached space for the first time in 1957, and the **first astronaut** was a Russian **dog** called Laika.

During **lift-off**, a large rocket generates as much **power** as **4,000 cars** or **500 jet fighter planes**.

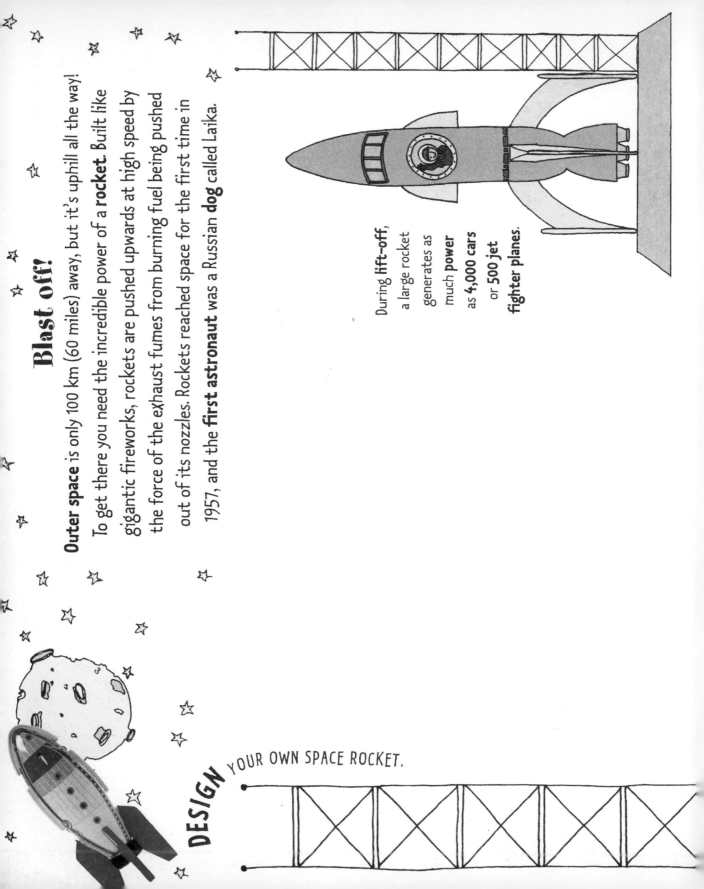

**DESIGN** YOUR OWN SPACE ROCKET.

**Astronauts** live in the top part of a rocket. The bottom half is made up of **stages,** which carry **fuel.** Once a stage has used up all its fuel, it is ejected and falls back to Earth.

# Toxic jumpers!

These rainforest-dwelling **amphibians** look colourful and friendly, but they are more **dangerous** than they seem. The bright patterns on the back of a poison dart frog tell predators not to eat it because it is **poisonous**. Rainforest tribes use the frogs' poison on the tips of their **blowpipe darts** when they hunt for food.

# One, two, three... jump!

Imagine sitting by an open door of a plane 4 km (2.5 miles) up and being told to jump – scary! For the first 60 seconds you're on your own, freefalling through the sky at speeds of between 190 and 290 kph (120 and 180 mph). At 760 m (0.5 mile) above the ground it's time to open your parachute. You'll land in 6–7 minutes, so be prepared!

Some say **skydiving** feels like **flying** rather than falling. If you are a beginner, you can **"tandem skydive"**, strapped to an instructor.

Experienced skydivers take part in brief, **death-defying** aerial displays. In 2008, **400 skydivers** joined up for 4 seconds to form a **spiral shape** – a freefall formation **world record**!

**DRAW** AND **COLOUR** SOME MORE SKYDIVERS.

DESIGN YOUR OWN WACKY
GLASS SCULPTURES.

# Sandy glass!

Did you know that **glass** is made of **sand**? Sand and other **chemicals** are mixed together, then **heated** to an extremely **high temperature**. The mixture melts and becomes a thick liquid. While it is **cooling** it can be bent into different shapes or poured out flat to make windows and mirrors. **Glass sculptures** can be made by twisting and stretching the glass into all sorts of shapes, and adding other pieces of **coloured glass** so that it all sticks together as it cools.

# It's cold out there!

Life can get **very chilly** in the Arctic regions around the **North Pole**, especially in winter. The **animals** that live there have special adaptations to help them live with the cold. Most have a **fur coat** or lots of feathers to help them **keep warm**. A type of **Arctic fish** has a special protein in its blood that stops it from **freezing solid**. Some animals spend many months asleep in **dens and burrows** when food gets scarce. Others go on long journeys **to escape** the bad weather and search for food.

**DRAW** SOME MORE ANIMALS ON THE ICE.

Arctic foxes and Arctic hares **turn from brown to white** in winter to help them **hide** from predators.

**WHAT** IS THE POLAR BEAR CHASING?

# Insects galore!

Some **900,000** different kinds of living insects have been identified and named, but scientists believe that there are still many more out there that haven't been discovered yet. Some say there could be more than **30 million** different kinds of insects in total!

It's been estimated that there are 10 quintillion individual insects alive at any one time – that's **a 10 with 18 zeros** after it!

Approximately **80%** of all the **animal species** in the world are insects!

**DRAW** SOME MORE INSECTS AND CREATE A **BUG FEST**!

**Earth's gravity** still has an effect on people in space — just not as much. If a **ladder connected** Earth and a **spacecraft in orbit**, and you climbed up it, you would **weigh 11% less** at the top! So if you weigh 27 kg (60 lb), you'd only weigh about 24 kg (53 lb) at the top of the ladder.

# Floating in space!

Did you know that **an astronaut is not really weightless?** Instead they are **just constantly falling** towards Earth, together with the spacecraft and everything inside it. So **how come they don't fall out of the sky?** Well, the Earth's surface is curved. As the spacecraft and its contents fall to Earth, they are also **travelling extremely fast "sideways".** The Earth's surface curves away from them as fast as they are falling so they end up **orbiting** the Earth and never reach the surface.

To remain in orbit, the **International Space Station** must travel about 28,000 kph (17,500 mph) – now that's fast!

**DRAW** THE ASTRONAUTS FLOATING AROUND THEIR **SPACE STATION.**

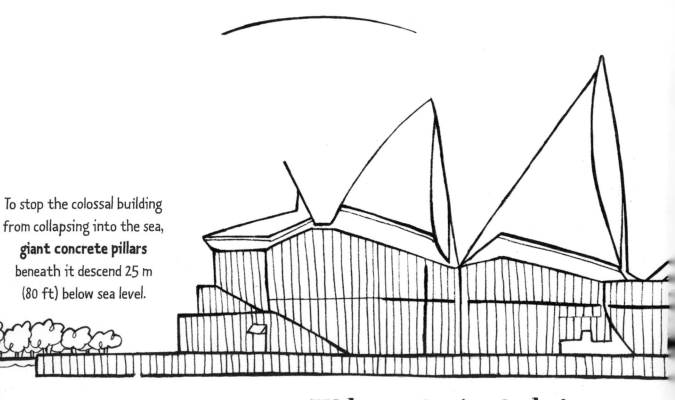

To stop the colossal building from collapsing into the sea, **giant concrete pillars** beneath it descend 25 m (80 ft) below sea level.

# Welcome to Australia!

**Sydney Opera House** is Australia's most famous building and a masterpiece of **modern architecture**. Surrounded by the glittering waters of beautiful **Sydney Harbour**, it resembles a **flotilla of boats**, their white sails filled by the wind. The "sails" consist of ten vast concrete **shells** covered with **gleaming white and cream tiles**. Inside are **seven halls**, the largest of which contains one of the **world's largest pipe organs**, with more than 10,000 pipes.

There are more than **1 million** glossy white and cream tiles on the roof of the Sydney Opera House.

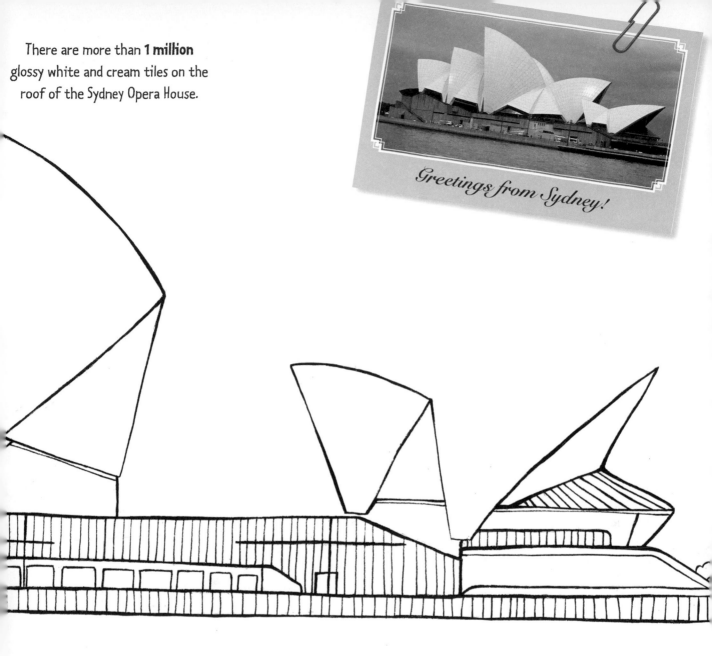

*Greetings from Sydney!*

**DRAW** MORE **BOATS** IN THE **HARBOUR**.

**DRAW** WHAT'S LIVING IN THE ROCKPOOL.

The **Goby Rock fish** has a **suction cup** on its underside, which it uses to **cling** onto rocks so it doesn't get **washed away** with the tide.

## It's a hard life!

One minute it's **low tide** and the sun is beating down and evaporating water from the **rockpool** shallows, making them saltier than usual; the next minute, it's **high tide**, huge waves are crashing down onto the pools, and the water temperature drops. These are the **daily living conditions** that any creature or plant living in a rockpool has to be able to cope with if it is to **survive**.

**DRAW** SOME MORE SKIERS AND SNOWBOARDERS - WHO WILL BE THE FIRST TO MAKE A JUMP?

# Nerves of steel!

Extreme skiing and snowboarding takes a lot of **nerve and skill**. An **extreme skier** can reach speeds between 200 and 250 kph (124 and 155 mph), and **extreme snowboarders** have been known to go as fast as 201 kph (125 mph)! Travelling this fast, they have to have their wits about them so they can **dodge obstacles** such as rocks, trees, and crevasses (tricky), **avoid avalanches** (almost impossible!), and be able to successfully complete **amazing jumps**!

**Avalanches** are incredibly powerful and **destructive**. Slabs of dry snow can reach speeds of 129 kph (80 mph) within 5 seconds of starting their **downward slide**.

**DESCRIBE** OR **DRAW** A TYPICAL DAY IN YOUR NOTEBOOK.

BURIED BY

...........Kinshou..........

**Spacecraft** have even taken time capsules into space for **future space travellers** to find. Voyager 1 and 2 have a gold-plated, copper phonograph record on board, containing pictures and sounds of **life on Earth**. It will take around **40,000 years** before the spacecraft reach another planetary system!

# Future treasures!

Have you ever thought about making a **time capsule** and leaving it for people to discover many years from now? Time capsules commonly contain **photos, diaries, and objects** so that future generations can have a "**snapshot**" of what life was like in the past. A time capsule in Nebraska, USA, has a **white pyramid** above ground to mark where it is buried. It has around **5,000 items** inside it – including **two cars**!

**DRAW** WHAT YOU WOULD STORE IN YOUR **TIME CAPSULE.**

# It's snowing!

It's always exciting when snow starts to fall. These fluffy **snowflakes** started life as miniscule **crystals of ice**, high up in the clouds. The crystals gradually join together to make heavier six-sided **clusters** that start to fall towards the ground. If the **air temperature** is **cold** enough, the clusters fall to Earth as snowflakes.

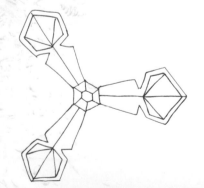

COMPLETE THE FALLING SNOWFLAKES.

# DRAW SNOWFLAKES OF YOUR OWN.

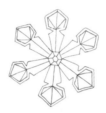

Snowflakes always have **six branches,** but they come in an endless **variety** of **patterns** and **sizes.** No two snowflakes are ever the same.

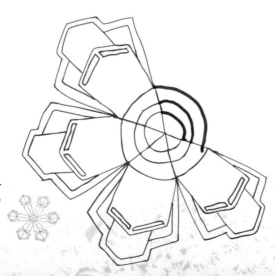

Most snowflakes are so **tiny** that we can only see their shapes through a **microscope.** The snow that arrives on the ground is usually groups of flakes clumped together.

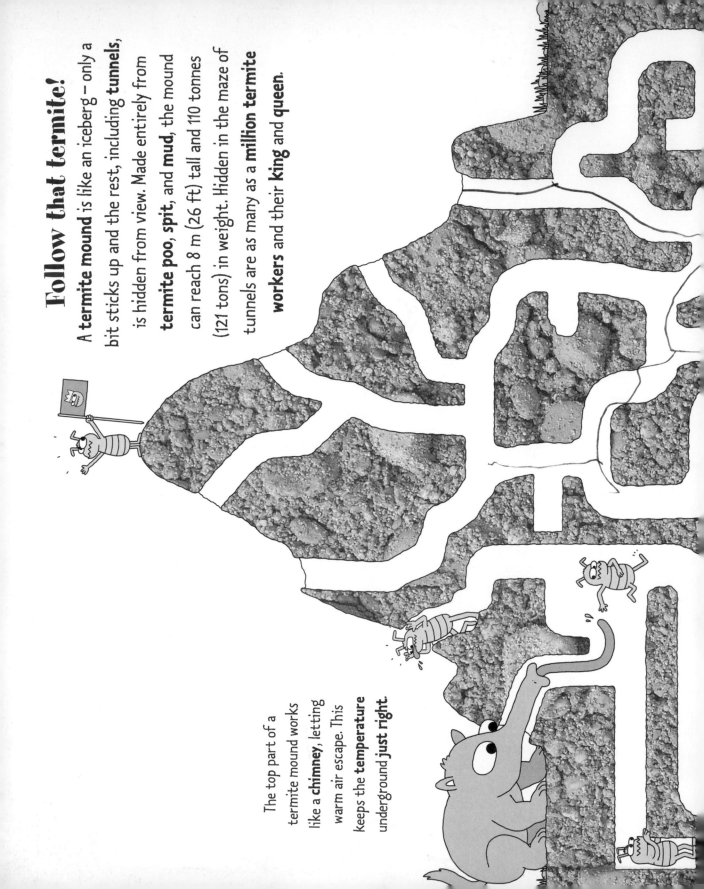

# Follow that termite!

A **termite mound** is like an iceberg – only a bit sticks up and the rest, including **tunnels**, is hidden from view. Made entirely from **termite poo**, **spit**, and **mud**, the mound can reach 8 m (26 ft) tall and 110 tonnes (121 tons) in weight. Hidden in the maze of tunnels are as many as a **million termite workers** and their **king** and **queen**.

The top part of a termite mound works like a **chimney**, letting warm air escape. This keeps the **temperature** underground **just right**.

FIND THE WAY TO THE **BOTTOM** OF THE **MOUND** AND BACK OUT OF THE **TOP**.

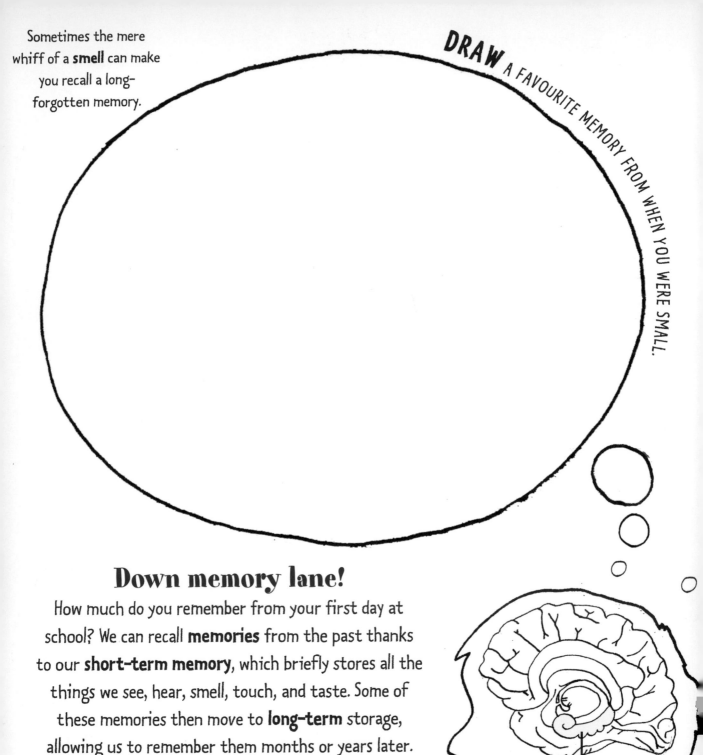

Sometimes the mere whiff of a **smell** can make you recall a long-forgotten memory.

## Down memory lane!

How much do you remember from your first day at school? We can recall **memories** from the past thanks to our **short-term memory**, which briefly stores all the things we see, hear, smell, touch, and taste. Some of these memories then move to **long-term** storage, allowing us to remember them months or years later. There isn't just one place in your **brain** where our memories are kept, but a part of the brain, called the **hippocampus**, plays a vital role in turning short-term memories into long-term ones.

Hippocampus

**DRAW** YOUR
EARLIEST MEMORY.

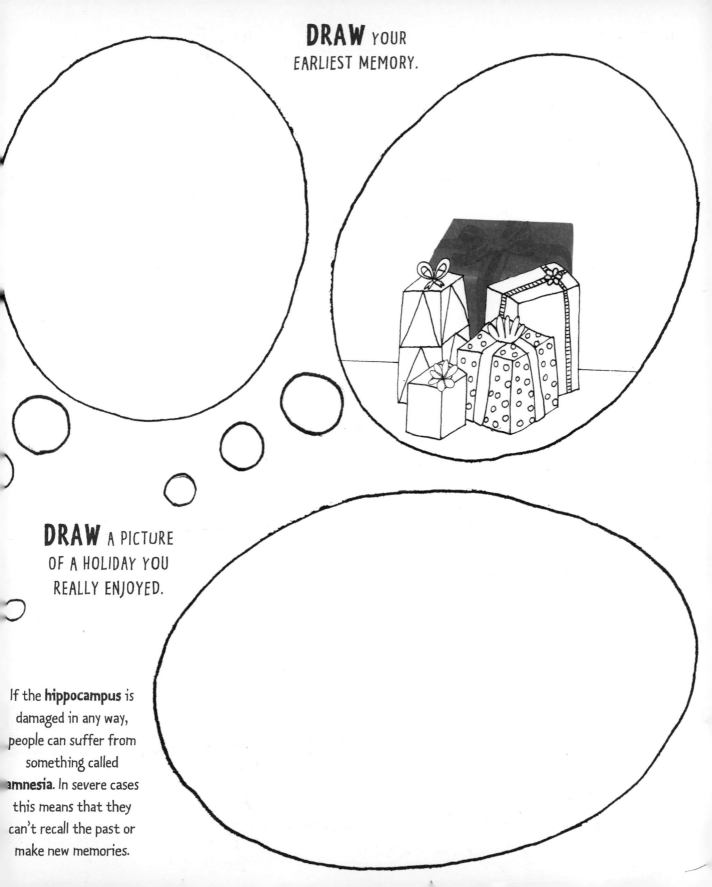

**DRAW** A PICTURE
OF A HOLIDAY YOU
REALLY ENJOYED.

If the **hippocampus** is
damaged in any way,
people can suffer from
something called
**amnesia**. In severe cases
this means that they
can't recall the past or
make new memories.

# Gaming world!

Things have certainly changed a lot since the first **video games** were **invented** in the 1970s. Today the games industry employs thousands of people worldwide and makes more than twice as much money as the film industry in the USA alone. It takes a team

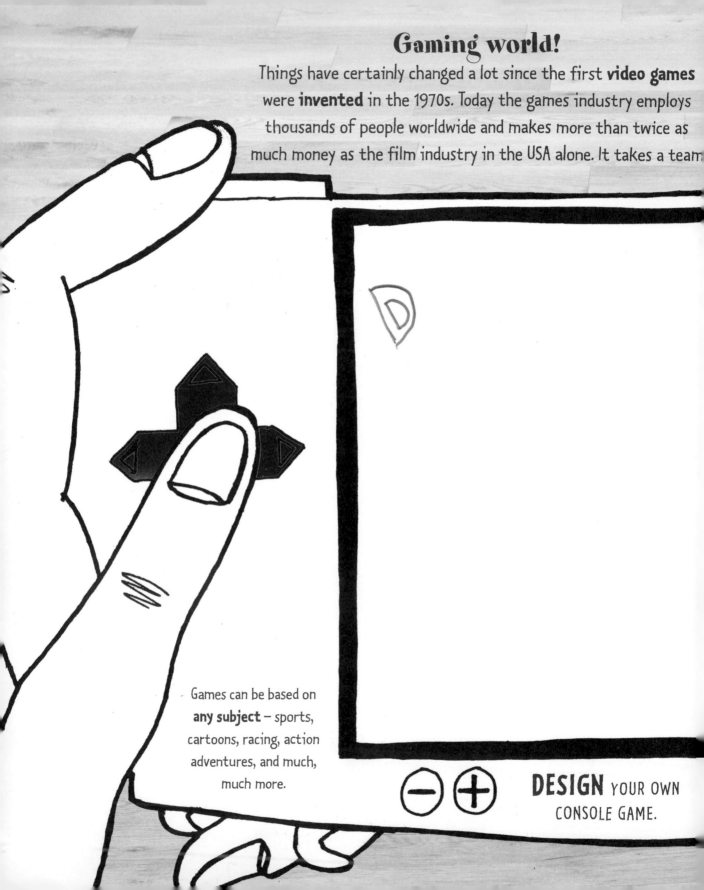

Games can be based on **any subject** – sports, cartoons, racing, action adventures, and much, much more.

**DESIGN** YOUR OWN CONSOLE GAME.

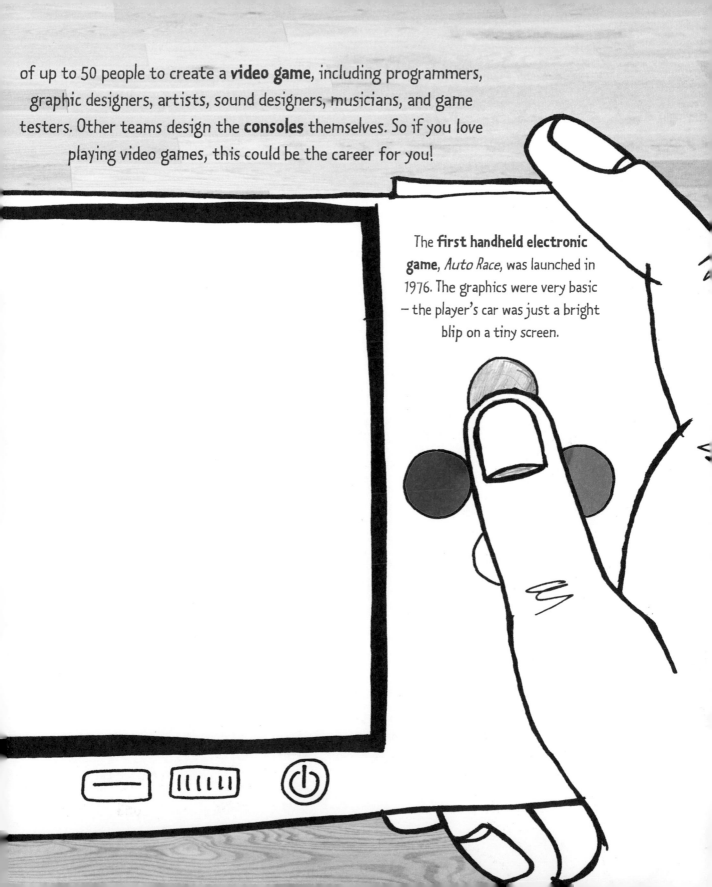

of up to 50 people to create a **video game**, including programmers, graphic designers, artists, sound designers, musicians, and game testers. Other teams design the **consoles** themselves. So if you love playing video games, this could be the career for you!

The **first handheld electronic game**, *Auto Race*, was launched in 1976. The graphics were very basic – the player's car was just a bright blip on a tiny screen.

Mount Everest is 8,848 m (29,035 ft) tall, and it is **still getting taller**! Every year it gets a few millimetres higher due to movements of the **Earth's crust**.

# On top of the world!

Intrepid **climbers** from all over the world travel to **Nepal** for the ultimate challenge – conquering **Mount Everest**, the **world's tallest mountain**. It's a dangerous climb, so dangerous that the area above 8,000 m (26,000 ft) is known as the **"death zone"**. Climbers have to battle with **high winds**, **sub-zero temperatures**, and **low oxygen levels**. But it's all worth it for the magic moment when they reach the **summit** and stand on the very top of the world!

DRAW MORE FEARLESS CLIMBERS.

Many climbers who get into difficulties on Everest are **rescued by helicopter**. In 2005 one helicopter set a record for the highest ever landing by touching down on the summit!

The **stripes** are not just fur deep – if you shaved a tiger, the **skin** would be striped underneath too!

**DRAW** THE TIGER'S STRIPES.

Do tigers

A tiger's **terrifying**, loud **roar** can be heard as far as three kilometres (two miles) away.

**DRAW** SOME MORE TIGERS PROWLING THROUGH THE GRASS.

## Prowling in the shadows!

Normally an animal's camouflage helps them to hide from predators, but a tiger's **stripy skin** helps it to hide from its **prey**. The lines break up the outline of its body, helping the tiger blend into shadows created by the long grass. This means it can **creep up on its victim** without being spotted. A tiger's stripes are as unique as fingerprints are to people; no two tigers have the same pattern.

DRAW YOUR OWN AMAZING EXPERIMENTS AND EXPLOSIONS.

Our **bodies** are full of chemical reactions. There are more than 100 trillion cells in the human body and **each cell** produces **thousands** of **chemical reactions**. That adds up to quite a lot!

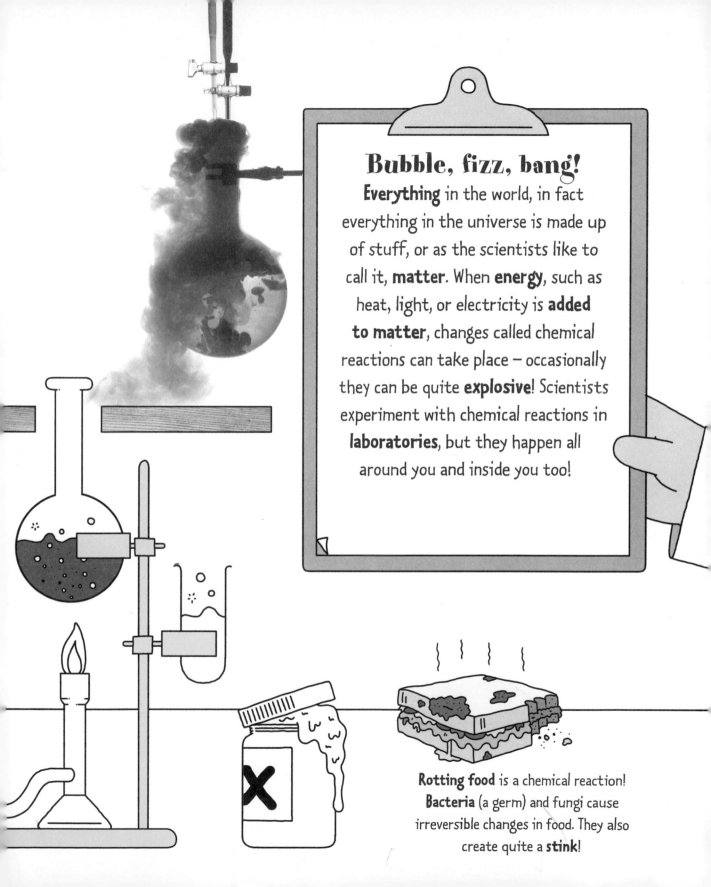

# Bubble, fizz, bang!

**Everything** in the world, in fact everything in the universe is made up of *stuff*, or as the scientists like to call it, **matter**. When **energy**, such as heat, light, or electricity is **added to matter**, changes called chemical reactions can take place – occasionally they can be quite **explosive**! Scientists experiment with chemical reactions in **laboratories**, but they happen all around you and inside you too!

**Rotting food** is a chemical reaction! **Bacteria** (a germ) and fungi cause irreversible changes in food. They also create quite a **stink**!

# Extremely dry!

The **Atacama Desert** in Chile, South America, is a very thirsty place. Situated high in the **Andes Mountains**, some weather stations there have never recorded a **single drop of rain**. The mountains are the reason for this. They are so high that rainclouds coming in from the Pacific Ocean are forced to drop their load of water on the coastal side of the mountains in order to rise over the tops. By the time the clouds have reached the Atacama on the other side, there is practically **no water** left.

Space scientists test their **space robots** in the Atacama Desert as the **landscape is similar to that of Mars.**

**DESIGN** YOUR OWN SPACE ROBOT.

**ADD** SOME MORE **SHAGGY** LLAMAS.

# Incredibly wet!

There are several contenders for the title of **wettest inhabited place** on Earth. It all depends on how you measure it. One of them is **Lloró** in Colombia. This town receives 13.3 m (44 ft) of rain spread throughout the year. Another contender is **Mawsynram** in India. This gets 11.8 m (39 ft), though most of this falls during the short **monsoon season.**

**Cloudbursts** can drop 10 cm (4 in) of rain in an hour.

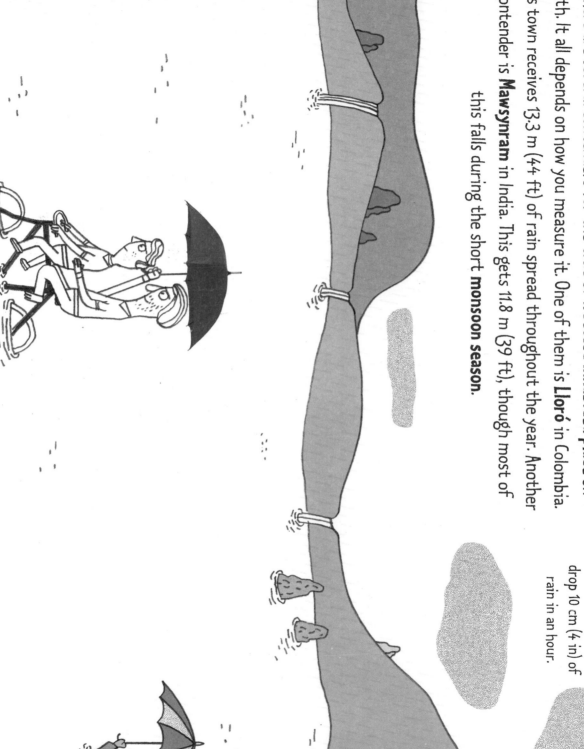

**DRAW** HOW YOU WOULD GET ACROSS THE FLOOD.

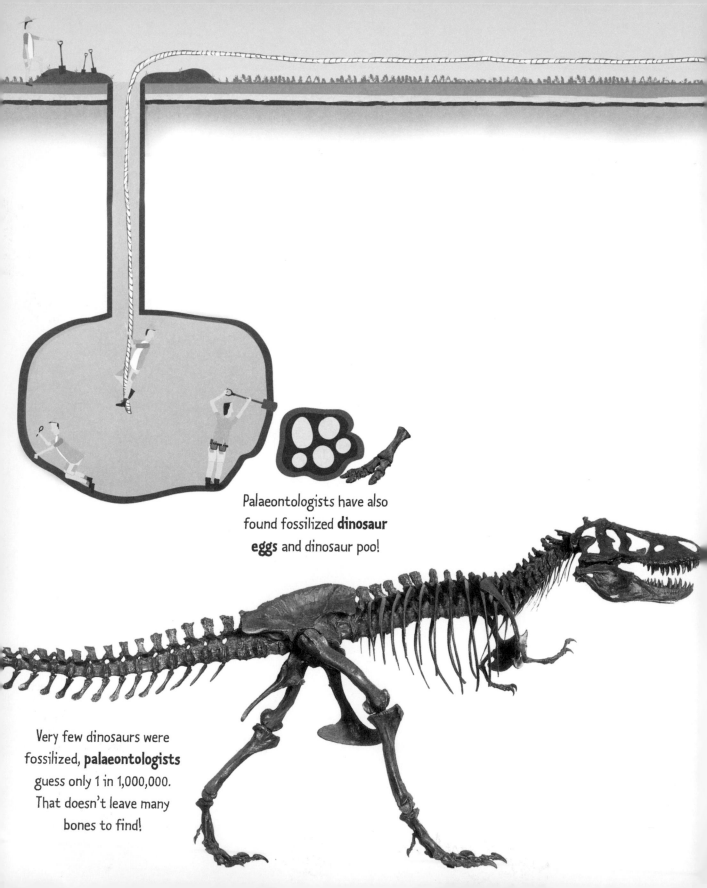

Palaeontologists have also found fossilized **dinosaur eggs** and dinosaur poo!

Very few dinosaurs were fossilized, **palaeontologists** guess only 1 in 1,000,000. That doesn't leave many bones to find!

# Buried bones!

Everything we have learnt about dinosaurs comes from their **fossilized remains**. Fossils need certain conditions to form. When a dead dinosaur gets covered in sand or mud, its bones are **preserved** and over millions of years the sand and mud turn to rock. The **bones** of the dead dinosaur **absorb** minerals and harden into fossils – ready for dino-seekers (palaeontologists) to find them.

DRAW SOME **FOSSILIZED BONES** FOR THE PALAEONTOLOGISTS TO DISCOVER.

# Viking attack!

If you had lived a thousand years ago, this is something you
would not have wanted to see – a boatful of scary **Vikings**!
These fierce warriors from **Scandinavia** terrorized people all
over Europe, **raiding** their towns and villages, **stealing** anything
valuable they could grab, and leaving a trail of **death and
destruction** behind them.

A Viking warrior wore a **metal helmet** and
carried a **shield**. He was armed with a **sword**,
**axe**, or **spear** and was not afraid to use it!

The Vikings crossed the sea in wooden ships, called **longboats**, powered by oars and a sail and decorated with a dragon's head.

**DRAW** MORE FEARSOME **FIGHTERS** TO COMPLETE THE **VIKING ARMY**.

DRAW AND COLOUR MORE BALLOONS

# Up, up, and away!

A **hot-air balloon** may not be the fastest ways to travel, but it is probably one of the most amazing! A **burner** under the balloon burns **propane gas**, which **heats the air** inside the balloon. As the air warms up, the balloon **rises**. To go higher, the pilot turns up the **flame**. To stop rising or lose height, he pulls a cord, which opens a **valve** at the top of the balloon, and allows some hot air to **escape**.

The **highest** a balloon has ever flown was in 2005 in **Bombay, India**. It went up 21,290 metres (69,852 ft) – that's 21 km (13 miles) high!

The first **passengers** of the very first hot-air balloon in 1783 were a **sheep**, a **cockerel**, and a **duck**!

DESIGN YOUR OWN BALLOON.

# Super-cool gadgets!

Have you ever wanted to be a **spy**? You'll need some cool gadgets to help you. How about sunglasses with a **hidden camera**, night-vision **goggles** for spying after dark, a voice-activated pen to record conversations, or a **roving robot** that can do the spying for you. What may appear to be a normal everyday object, may in fact be a spy **gadget**, so keep a lookout!

A spy is a person employed to **collect secret information**, known as **"intelligence"**, about another country's government, military, or industries.

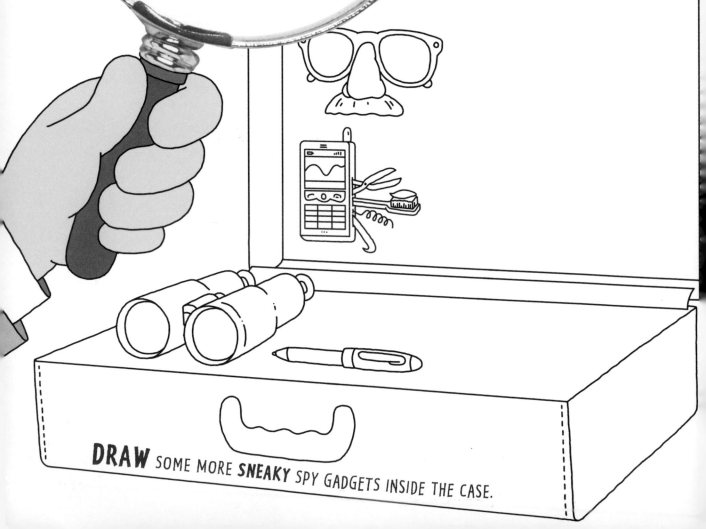

**DRAW** SOME MORE **SNEAKY** SPY GADGETS INSIDE THE CASE.

# DESIGN AN ALL-SEEING, ALL-HEARING, COOL SPY ROBOT.

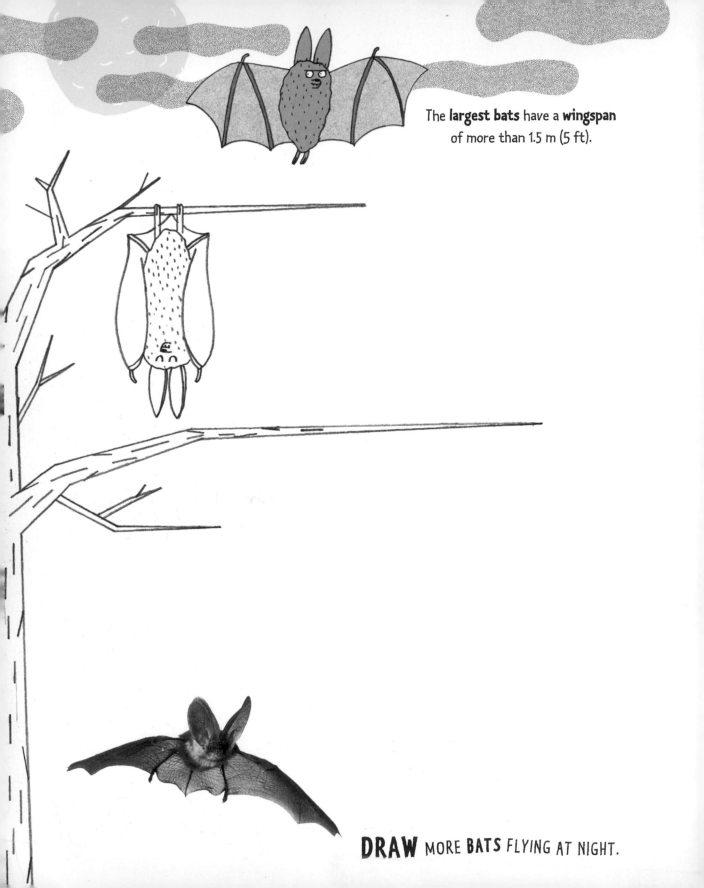

The **largest bats** have a **wingspan** of more than 1.5 m (5 ft).

**DRAW** MORE **BATS** FLYING AT NIGHT.

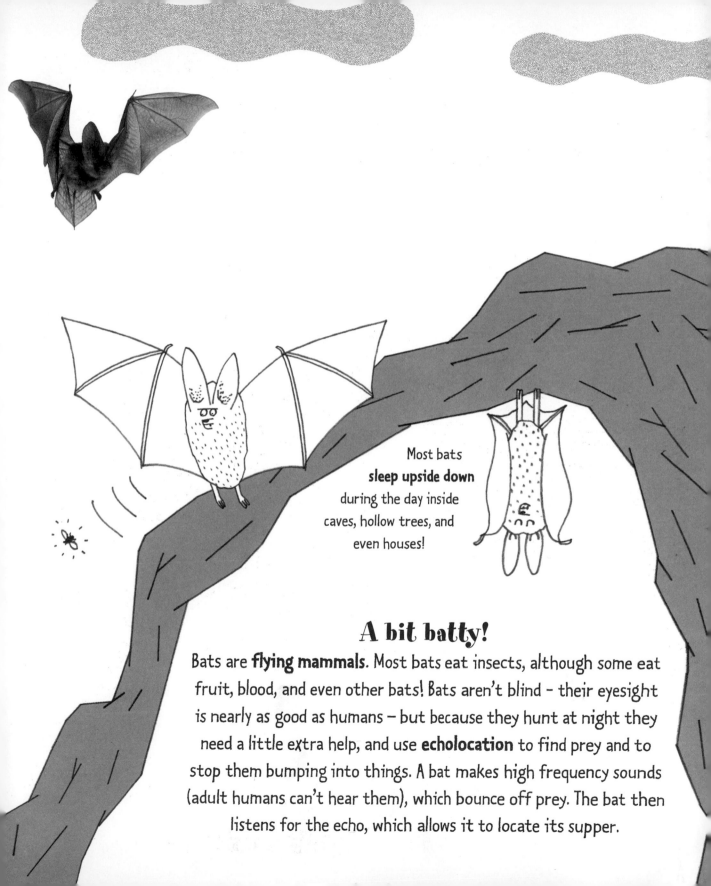

Most bats **sleep upside down** during the day inside caves, hollow trees, and even houses!

# A bit batty!

Bats are **flying mammals**. Most bats eat insects, although some eat fruit, blood, and even other bats! Bats aren't blind - their eyesight is nearly as good as humans – but because they hunt at night they need a little extra help, and use **echolocation** to find prey and to stop them bumping into things. A bat makes high frequency sounds (adult humans can't hear them), which bounce off prey. The bat then listens for the echo, which allows it to locate its supper.

They are two main types of
curved mirror, **concave** ones that
curve in and **convex** that bulge
out. To know which is which,
just remember caves go in,
as do concave mirrors!

# Bendy reflections!

Have you ever been in a **hall of mirrors** at an amusement park or circus?
The mirrors are designed to create **strange and bizarre reflections**.
Some mirrors make you really tall, while others make you really short.
How do the mirrors work? The mirrors **aren't flat** like the ones you have
at home. Instead they are **warped and curved** so they **reflect** light rays
back at **strange angles**, creating the fun and weird reflections.

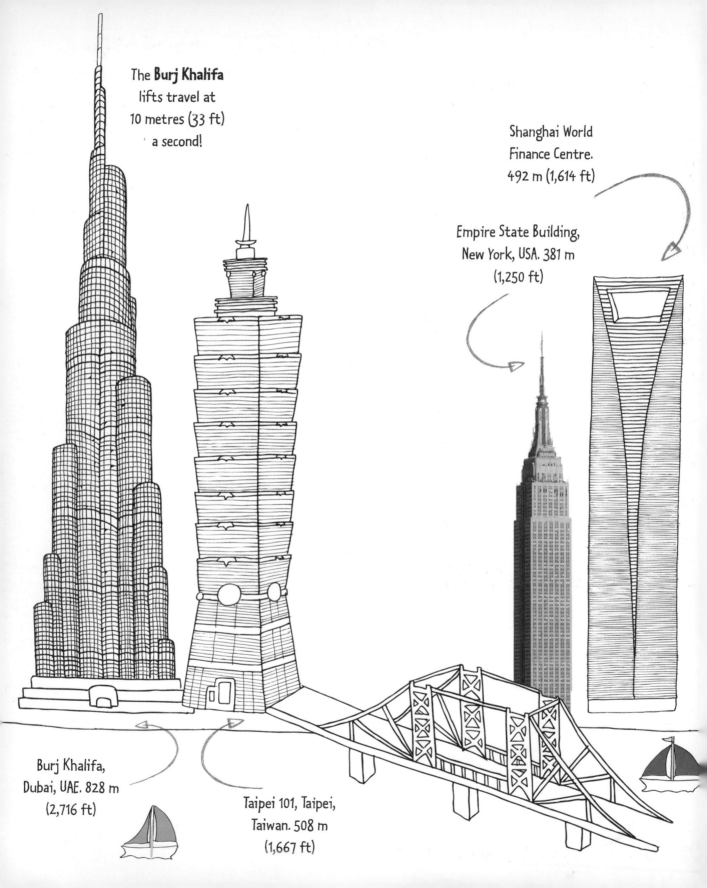

The **Burj Khalifa** lifts travel at 10 metres (33 ft) a second!

Shanghai World Finance Centre. 492 m (1,614 ft)

Empire State Building, New York, USA. 381 m (1,250 ft)

Burj Khalifa, Dubai, UAE. 828 m (2,716 ft)

Taipei 101, Taipei, Taiwan. 508 m (1,667 ft)

# Higher and higher and higher...

There have always been **tall buildings** – just think of the **Egyptian pyramids**. However, until the mid-19th century, a building's height was limited by the **number of stairs** people were willing to climb and how much **weight** brick walls could support. Two inventions changed all that – the **lift** (no more stairs – whoopee!) and the use of a **steel frame** to **support the building**. Since then, buildings have rocketed **skywards**!

The Shard, London,
United Kingdom.
310 m (1,016 ft)

Petronas Towers,
Kuala Lumpur,
Malaysia. 452 m
(1,482 ft)

**DESIGN** YOUR OWN **SKYSCRAPERS** – THE SKY'S THE LIMIT!

# Incredibly cold!

Imagine a place where pen ink **freezes** and metal sticks to skin. Welcome to **Oymyakon**, the **coldest inhabited village** on Earth! Situated in **Siberia, Russia**, the temperature here has been known to go as low as -71.2°C (-96.16°F). Winter lasts for **nine months** of the year and children are not allowed outside to play for more than **twenty minutes** at a time because the **extreme cold** could damage their lungs.

Strangely enough, Oymyakon is named after a nearby **hot spring!**

**DRAW** YOURSELF AND YOUR FRIENDS PLAYING OUTSIDE — WRAP UP WARM!

# Extremely hot!

Dallol in Ethiopia currently holds the record for the world's **highest average temperature**. Most days the thermometer reaches 34°C (94°F), but it can go as high as 64°C (148°F) in summer. Only a few people live here – it's miles from anywhere, there are no proper roads, and abandoned cars that have broken down are still awaiting recovery! The only reliable transport is a camel.

The landscape is brightly coloured red, yellow, and white from the mineral salts that evaporate from **volcanic springs** underground.

**COLOUR** THE LANDSCAPE IN REDS, YELLOWS, AND WHITE.

**DRAW** AN ERUPTING VOLCANO AND SOME CAMELS.

It took the **crew** of a steam train nearly **three hours** to generate enough steam to get the train moving.

**DRAW** THE MISSING WAGON — WHAT'S INSIDE THEM ALL?

# All aboard!

The first trains were called **steam trains** because they were **powered** by steam and belched out great clouds of **steam** and **smoke**. The engine car at the front contained a huge **coal fire** that was used to boil water and turn it into steam, which then travelled through pipes and pushed **pistons** (rods) that turned the wheels round. Steam engines generated fantastic power – enough to pull a long row of heavy carriages.

**DESIGN** YOUR OWN TRAIN.

# Terrors from the deep!

**Life on Earth** most likely started in **the oceans**. There are several **millions of species** of animals that live in the oceans, some we haven't yet discovered because the oceans are so **vast and very, very deep**. Some of the fish that live in the oceans are very **strange and unique**.

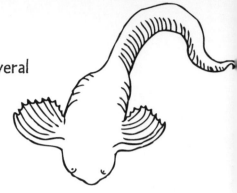

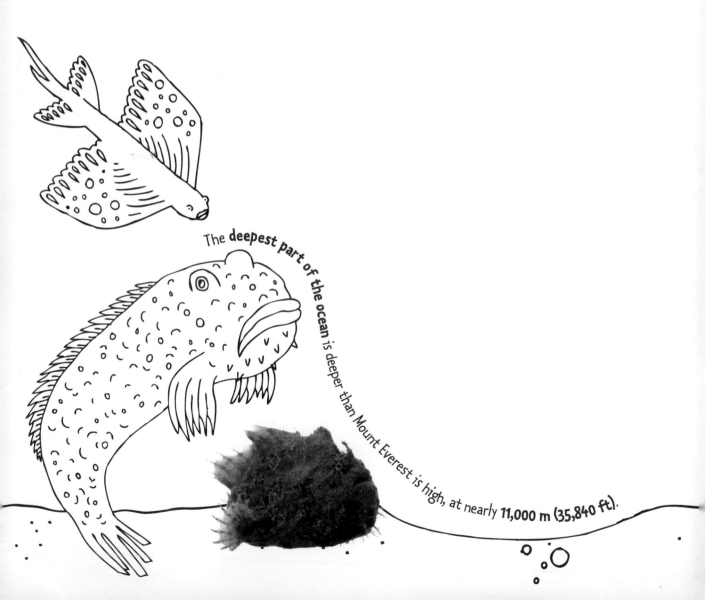

The **deepest part of the ocean** is deeper than Mount Everest is high, at nearly **11,000 m (35,840 ft)**.

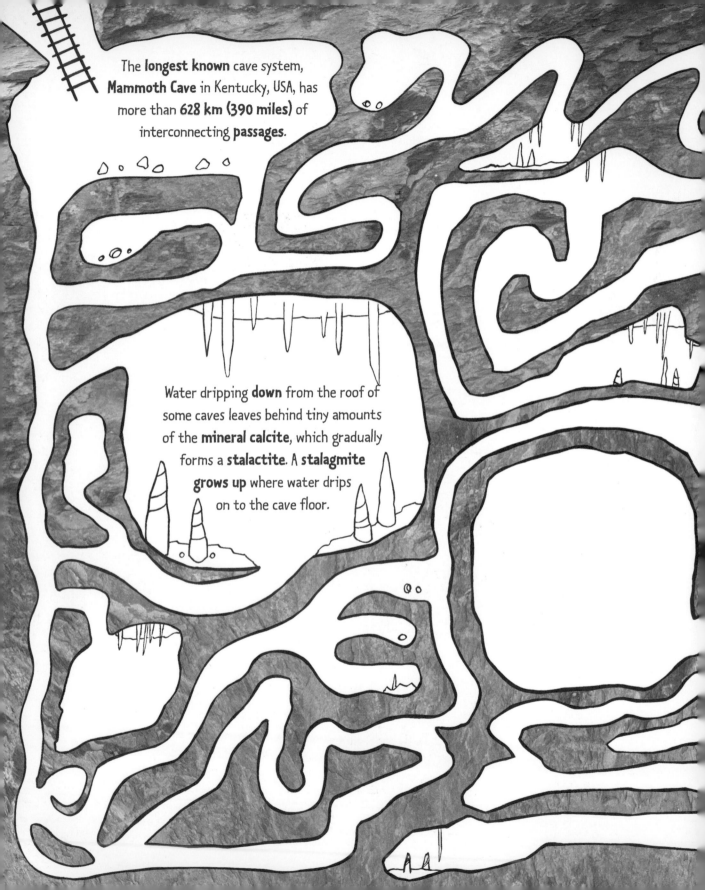

The **longest known** cave system, **Mammoth Cave** in Kentucky, USA, has more than **628 km (390 miles)** of interconnecting **passages**.

Water dripping **down** from the roof of some caves leaves behind tiny amounts of the **mineral calcite**, which gradually forms a **stalactite**. A **stalagmite grows up** where water drips on to the cave floor.

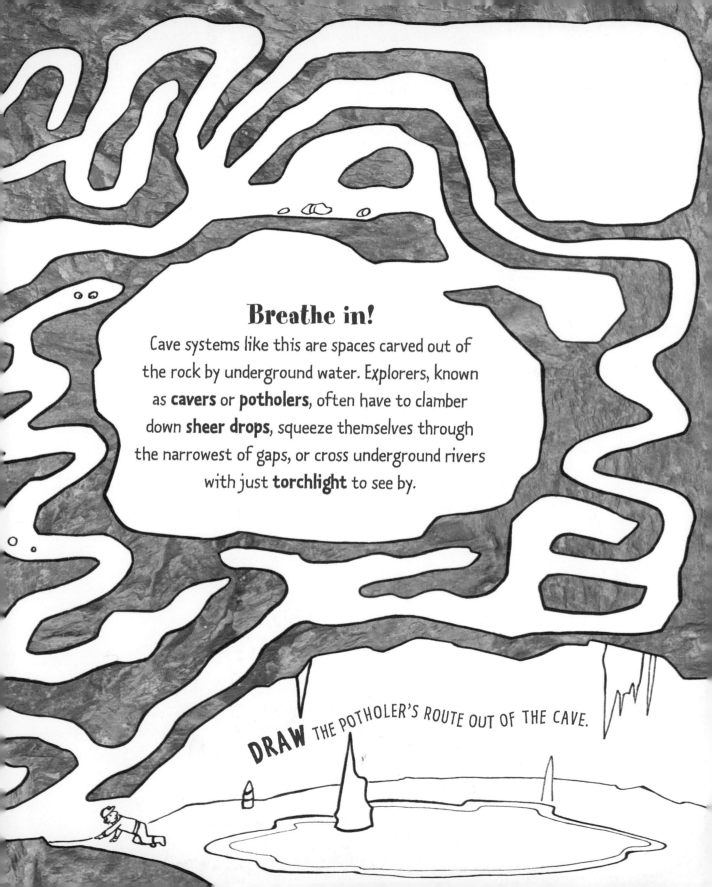

# Breathe in!

Cave systems like this are spaces carved out of the rock by underground water. Explorers, known as **cavers** or **potholers**, often have to clamber down **sheer drops**, squeeze themselves through the narrowest of gaps, or cross underground rivers with just **torchlight** to see by.

DRAW THE POTHOLER'S ROUTE OUT OF THE CAVE.

In the **future**, there will need to be rules about driving the **sky highways** – you can't paint white lines or have crash barriers up there!

**COMPLETE** THIS CAR SO THAT IT CAN FLY HIGH!

Curtiss Autoplane 1917

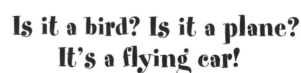

# Is it a bird? Is it a plane? It's a flying car!

People have been fascinated by the idea of flying cars for years. The **Curtiss Autoplane**, with its removable wings and tail, was designed in 1917 – however it hopped rather than flew! Some recent designs include the **Moller M400 Skycar**, designed to fly up to 579 kph (360 mph), the gyroplane car **PAL-V**, with speeds of up to 180 kph (112 mph), and the **Terrafugia Transition**, which has fold-away wings and speeds of 172–185 kph (105–115 mph).

The leaves these ants are carrying aren't for eating. Instead, the ants **munch the leaves** up and **mix them** with their saliva. The ants then eat the **fungus** that grows on the mixture.

**COMPLETE** AND **COLOUR** THE LINE OF ANTS.

# As strong as an...ant?

A 1 cm ($^1/_3$ inch) long **leaf-cutter ant** can climb 30 m (100 ft) trees, cut off pieces of leaf (which can weigh 50 times its body weight), then, following a special scent trail, **carry** these back to its **underground nest**. Imagine the equivalent for people – it would mean walking several kilometres with a medium-sized van on our back!

An **ant's nest** can be the size of a **small car**!

# Technical trainers!

Designing **trainers** is a complicated business. Obviously they have to look cool, but that's only part of the story. Each style is carefully designed, using the latest materials, for a **specific sport**. Track athletes, for example, use **spikes** – incredibly light shoes with a thin rubber sole, a top made of mesh, and special spikes on the bottom to help them grip the track.

High-top shoes were originally designed for **basketball**. They come high up over the ankle to support the joint as the player sprints and jumps.

**DESIGN** YOUR OWN TRAINER PATTERN AND LOGO.

In 2007, Ken Courtney, US fashion designer, made 5 pairs of **gold-dipped** high-top basketball shoes. They sold for £2,702 (US $4,053) a pair, making them **the world's most expensive** trainers!

The United Kingdom has the most CCTV cameras per citizen, with 4.2 million cameras – that's **one CCTV camera for every 15 people!**

**DRAW** WHAT IS HAPPENING ON THE MONITORS.

According to statistics, a person can be caught on camera up to **300 times** a day!

# They're watching you!

Video cameras are used around the world to help us watch and observe. These video cameras form a system called **Closed-circuit television (CCTV)**. CCTV cameras are used for different reasons, from **protecting valuables and property**, observing the public, and even in factories to **monitor procedures** that are too dangerous for humans to be near. CCTV is used to **prevent crimes**, but it is also seen as an **invasion** of people's **privacy**.

# What's up there?

If you look up into a clear **night sky**, it's amazing how many different things you can see. Using just your eyes or a telescope, you can spot **the Moon**, hundreds of **stars**, and sometimes even a **shooting star**. Look out for **planets** such as Venus or Jupiter, too. Planets are much closer to us than the stars, so they look like **small, bright discs** in the sky. You may also see some **slow-moving** specks of light. These are man-made **satellites** that circle our planet.

A **shooting star** is not really a star at all, but a **meteor**. It is a lump of rock or other debris from space that burns up as it enters Earth's **atmosphere**.

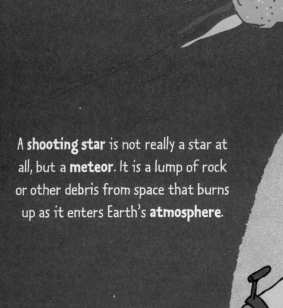

DRAW MORE STARS AND PLANETS IN THE **NIGHT SKY**.

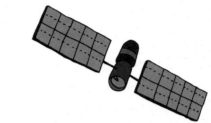

The easiest **satellite** to spot is the **International Space Station**, because it is very big. It completes an **orbit** of the Earth every 90 minutes. It is often mistaken for a **UFO!**

# Giant wheels!

Monster trucks are normal **pick-up** style trucks that have been **customized** with **beefed-up engines** and **giant tyres**. Monster trucks are powerful so they can drive over obstacles, such as dirt ramps and normal road cars. Monster trucks can be up to 3.5 m (12 ft) high – that's as high as you, with two of your friends standing on your shoulders! With **giant wheels** and lots of crazy stunts, the monster trucks need really big and **powerful suspensions**, but even then it's a bumpy ride!

Monster trucks are **customized** in lots of different ways ranging from **colourful patterns** to sculpted dinosaur designs!

A new set of **giant tyres** can cost around £8,000 (US $12,500) – that's a lot of pocket money!

# DESIGN YOUR OWN MEGA MONSTER TRUCKS!

**DRAW** SOMETHING
**FANTASTIC**
TO FINISH THE SECTION.

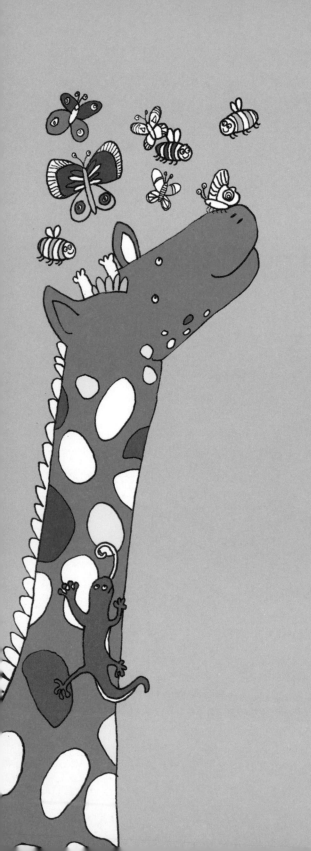

# DOODLEPEDIA
# ANIMAL ANTICS

DRAW MORE PENGUINS PLAYING AND SLIDING ON THE SLOPES.

SOUTH POLE

# Penguin playtime

Careful, it's slippery! Penguins are excellent swimmers and spend most of their time in the water. Although they can walk on their flippers, on slippery snow and ice it's quicker for penguins to slide down hills on their belly. Wouldn't you rather toboggan, too?

**Adélie Penguins** are mostly black with a white front.

**Chinstrap Penguins** look like they are wearing a black hat!

**Emperor Penguins** are the biggest of all penguins.

**COLOUR** IN THE DIFFERENT KINDS OF PENGUIN.

Penguin mums and dads raise their chicks together.

# Cheeky chipmunks

Chipmunks sleep underground through the cold winter months. But instead of living off stored body fat like many other animals, they gather food in their burrows. They then sleep nearby in their nest, waking every few days to have a snack to keep themselves going.

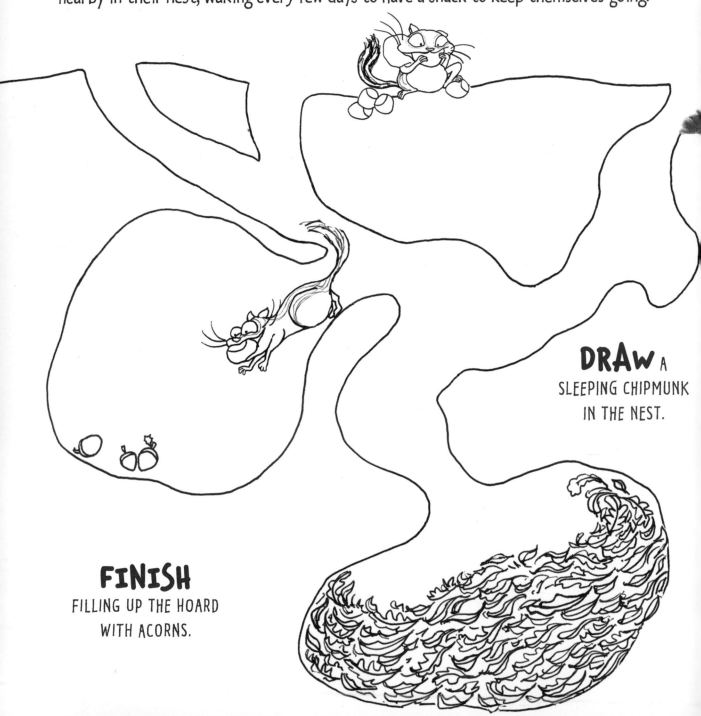

**DRAW** A SLEEPING CHIPMUNK IN THE NEST.

**FINISH** FILLING UP THE HOARD WITH ACORNS.

# COLOUR

THE CHIPMUNKS AND
THEIR ACORNS.

Chipmunks carry
acorns in special pouches
in their cheeks.

A chipmunk can
collect as many as
165 acorns a day.

# Pretty polly

Parrotfish have an important job – they keep reefs healthy by scraping away material that builds up on the surface of the coral. However, in doing this, they sometimes break off small pieces of coral. These pass through the gut of the fish and out the other end as white coral sand.

**DRAW** PATTERNS ON THE PARROTFISH.

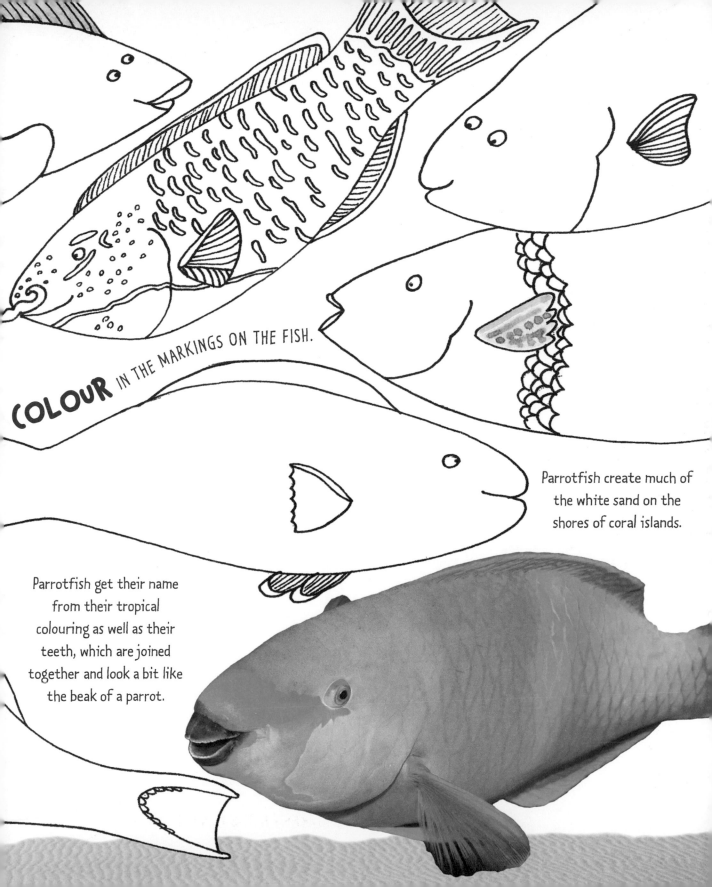

COLOUR IN THE MARKINGS ON THE FISH.

Parrotfish create much of the white sand on the shores of coral islands.

Parrotfish get their name from their tropical colouring as well as their teeth, which are joined together and look a bit like the beak of a parrot.

# Ear, ear!

Elephants are the biggest land animals. They can weigh up to 10 tonnes, or as much as 10 cars! There are three species (types) of elephant: African savanna elephants and African forest elephants live in Africa and Indian elephants live in Asia. One way to tell them apart is by their ears – African elephants have bigger ones.

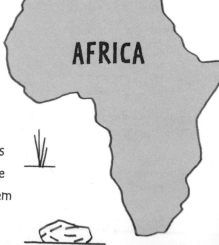

AFRICA

Look at this African elephant's ears – they're shaped a bit like Africa! On hot days he flaps them to create a cooling breeze.

Indian elephants have smaller ears that are shaped a bit like India.

INDIA

**DRAW** THE EARS ON THE ELEPHANTS TO SHOW WHETHER THEY'RE AFRICAN OR INDIAN.

# Spider webs

Spiders make their webs everywhere – in trees, bushes, and even in people's homes. Spiders use their web to catch insects. Insects either get tangled in the web, or they trip over the threads. This tells the spider to run out and catch the insect. Spiders spin the silk that the web is made from. It comes out of openings called spinnerets near their bottom!

**Tangle webs** can look a bit messy!

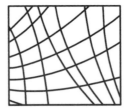

**Spiral orb webs** are round in shape.

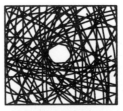

**Funnel webs** form a tube-like tunnel.

**Sheet webs** can cover large areas.

DRAW MORE SPIDERS SPINNING WEBS.

# Dolphin School

Although dolphins in marine-life centres often perform amazing tricks like swimming on their tail, dolphins in the wild rarely do. That is, unless someone teaches them to. When a bottlenose dolphin was released into the wild off the coast of Australia, scientists were surprised to discover many other dolphins soon performing the same tricks it had learned in captivity. The dolphin had taught its friends!

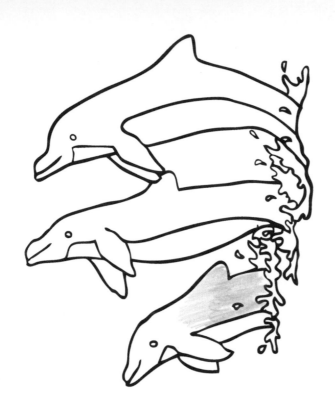

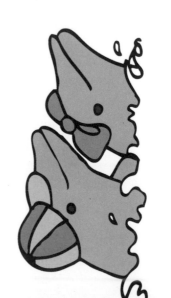

Dolphins are considered to be one of the world's most intelligent animals.

**DRAW** MORE DOLPHINS PERFORMING THE TRICKS THEY'VE LEARNED.

Bottlenose dolphins get their name from their short, bottle-like beak.

FIND AND COLOUR
THE RACCOONS.

COLOUR THE MAPLE
LEAVES IN AUTUMNAL
COLOURS.

# Peekaboo!

**Maple trees** are found all over the Northern Hemisphere, especially North America. The large maple leaves turn bright shades of **red** and **gold** in the autumn. These forests are full of **wildlife**. One inhabitant is the **raccoon**, a black and white **mammal** with a dog–like face and a long **bushy tail**. These mischievous animals have a patch of black fur around their eyes that makes them look like masked bandits!

The **largest maple leaf** was found by a boy in Canada. It reached 36 cm (13 in) wide and 29 cm (11 in) in length! That's **three times** as big as your head!

# Bowerbird's love nest

To impress a lady, give her... a bit of blue string? It might seem strange to us, but some bowerbird males attract females by building a bower (shelter) and decorating it with blue objects that they've found. And the ladies just love it!

Bowerbirds decorate their bower with man-made objects like bits of plastic and metal, as well as natural ones such as flowers and feathers.

FEMALE

# DRAW AND COLOUR

MORE BLUE OBJECTS TO HELP THIS
MALE ATTRACT A MATE.

Bowerbirds build
their U-shaped bower
out of sticks.

MALE

# Brown bears' feast

Brown bears love salmon, and have found a clever way to go fishing. They just stand in a river, wait for fish to swim by, and then grab them in their teeth or paws. Sometimes they even catch salmon leaping out of the water!

Brown bears sleep through the winter, so in autumn, they need to eat lots and lots of food to keep them going for all that time.

**DRAW** MORE SALMON JUMPING OUT OF THE RIVER.

## BEWARE OF THE BEARS

Bears sometimes dive in to catch
fish swimming under water.

DRAW MORE CAPUCHIN MONKEYS BREAKING OPEN FRUIT.

The stone "hammers" used by the capuchins can weigh up to 1.7kg (3.7lbs) – that's half the monkey's weight!

Young capuchin monkeys learn to break open fruit by watching older monkeys do it. Monkey see, monkey do.

# Monkey business

Capuchin monkeys are very clever and know how to break into the hardest fruit. If the fruit is too hard to open using their hands and teeth, they use tools! First they find somewhere to place the fruit so that it will not move. Then they strike it with a stone to split it open. Dinner is served!

**DRAW** MORE GECKOS CLIMBING UP AND DOWN THE WINDOW.

# Gluey geckos

Do geckos have superpowers? It's easy to think they do as they can walk up almost any surface, including walls and windows. In fact, their superpower is their specialized feet. The bottoms of their toes are covered in tiny hair-like bumps that can cling to the smallest ridge, allowing the gecko to hang on.

The tiny bumps on a gecko's toes allow it to climb up walls and windows.

Geckos eat insects, hunting them in places most other animals can't reach.

# Living on land

Land creatures come in all shapes and sizes. This is no surprise because the area of land they come from can be very different. Imagine living in a tropical rainforest, on a high mountain, in the frozen Arctic, or in a hot, dry desert. There's one thing all the animals have in common — each animal is perfectly suited to the place where it lives.

**FIND** THE CREATURE THAT SHOULDN'T BE ON LAND.

**COLOUR** ALL THE DIFFERENT LAND ANIMALS.

# Dressed crab

When they need to hide from predators, dresser crabs know just where to go – to the dressing-up box! Dresser crabs can blend in with their surroundings by attaching nearby objects to their body. They can do this because they have areas on their shell that stick a bit like Velcro.

**DRAW** MORE OBJECTS FOR THE DRESSER CRAB TO CHOOSE ITS OUTFIT FROM.

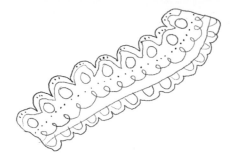

Dresser crabs have been known to wear bits of seaweed, coral, and even sea anemones. How fabulous!

**DRAW** WHAT THE DRESSER CRAB IS WEARING TO HIDE ITSELF.

If you get sprayed by a skunk, the smell can stay on you for several days.

DRAW MORE SKUNKS SPRAYING.

# You've been skunked!

Eurgh, what's that smell? It's worse than rotten eggs – it's a skunk! When skunks are frightened, they defend themselves by spraying strong, horrible scent from a gland under their tail. Before they spray, skunks give a warning. They stamp their feet and lift up their tail. Some skunks even do a handstand. You've been warned!

Skunks have very good aim. They can can hit a target up to 15m (50ft) away.

# Fly fishers

How does a fish hunt for food? With a water pistol, of course! The amazing archerfish catches insects from plants that overhang the water. It knocks them off with a jet of water produced by pressing its tongue against the roof of its mouth and quickly closing the gill covers. It can hit its target from a distance of about 1.5m (5ft)!

**DRAW** THE WATER SQUIRTS FROM THE FISH TO THE INSECTS.

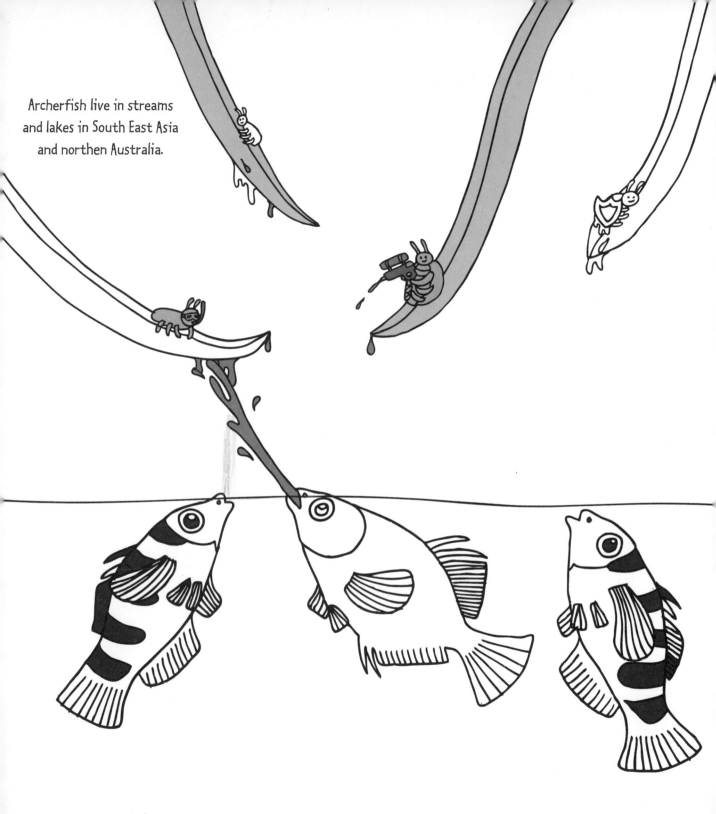

Archerfish live in streams and lakes in South East Asia and northen Australia.

**ADD** BANDS TO THE FISH AND FINISH COLOURING THE PICTURE.

# Dancing lemurs

If you ever go down to Madagasgar, you might see lemurs dancing! Most lemurs live in the trees, and leap from branch to branch. If the trees are too far apart the lemurs come down and cross the ground with a sideways jump-hop. At the same time, they hold their arms held out to the sides so it looks like they're dancing!

Madagascar is an island off the coast of Africa. On our globe, it's coloured in red.

**DRAW** MORE LEMURS DANCING ON THE GROUND.

Can you guess why this is called a
ring-tailed lemur?

# Scramble to the sea!

When a **mother sea turtle** is ready to **lay her eggs,**
she swims ashore, and lays and **buries her eggs in a hole** on
a sandy beach. Once she's laid them all, she crawls back
into the sea. After hatching, it may take the **baby turtles**
three or more days to dig their way out of the nest, then it's
a quick **night-time scramble** down the beach and off to sea!

A baby turtle has a **small
horn** on its head, called an
**egg tooth**, which it uses
to break out of the egg.

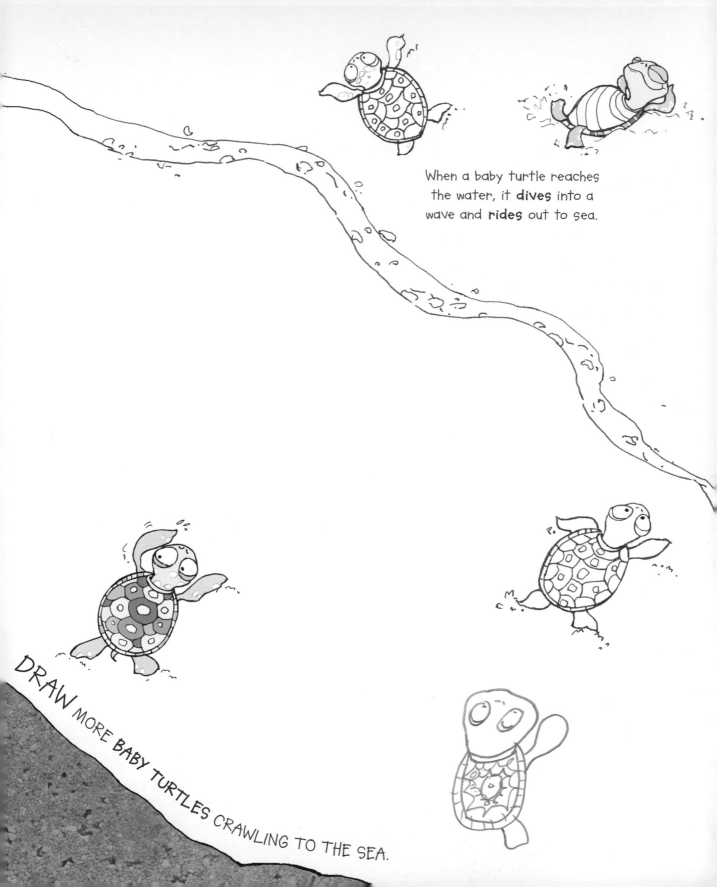

When a baby turtle reaches the water, it **dives** into a wave and **rides** out to sea.

DRAW MORE BABY TURTLES CRAWLING TO THE SEA.

# Dung beetle race

All dung beetles deserve a medal. They help keep the planet clean by eating dung (animal poo). Dung beetles known as "rollers" make balls out of the dung. They roll the balls to a place where they can be buried to eat later or used to lay their eggs in. Rollers need to roll their balls quickly, or they might be stolen by other dung beetles!

Dung beetles called "dwellers" live in a pile of dung.

**DRAW** MORE DUNG BEETLES IN THE RACE.

Dung beetles can roll a ball that is up to 10 times their own weight.

"Tunneller" beetles dig a tunnel under the dung to bury it where they find it.

# Stick it out!

Giraffes are very good at reaching leaves high up. First, they can grow to be up to 5.5m (18ft) tall – as tall as a two-storey building! Second, their very long tongue gives them extra reach. It can extend to up to 45cm (18in), or the length of 3 bananas!

Giraffes prefer to eat acacia leaves. They use their tongue and teeth to strip them from branches.

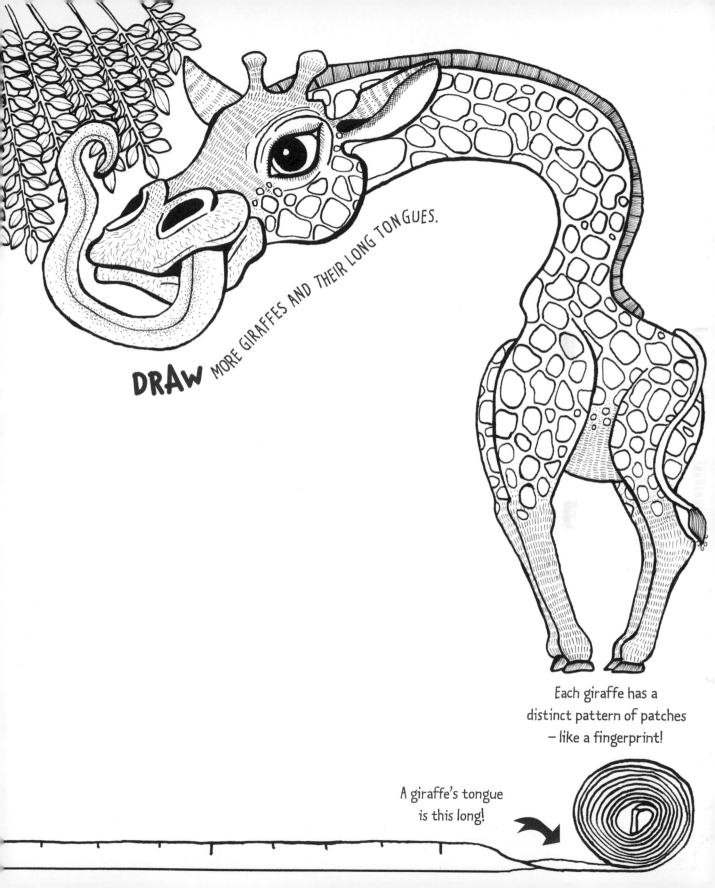

**DRAW** MORE GIRAFFES AND THEIR LONG TONGUES.

Each giraffe has a
distinct pattern of patches
– like a fingerprint!

A giraffe's tongue
is this long!

# Climbing goats

When people climb mountains, they need all kinds of equipment like ropes and axes. When mountain goats do it, they just use their specially shaped hooves. The hooves have a hard outer shell and a rubbery middle that works a bit like a suction cup to grip the ground with every step.

Mountain goats eat plants that grow on the mountains. These include grasses, herbs, and low-growing shrubs.

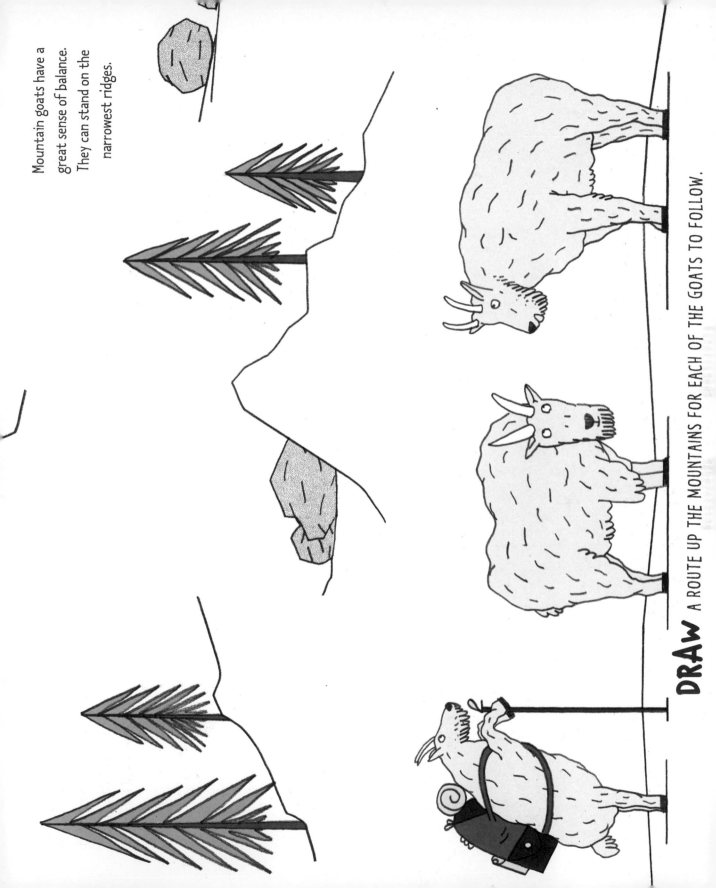

Mountain goats have a great sense of balance. They can stand on the narrowest ridges.

**DRAW** A ROUTE UP THE MOUNTAINS FOR EACH OF THE GOATS TO FOLLOW.

# kitten games

Kittens love to play – with their brothers and sisters and their toys. Playing is fun and it really improves their hunting skills. If you tie a toy to piece of string and dangle it in front of your kitten, it will stalk and pounce on the "prey". These kittens are hunting balls of yarn.

**CONNECT** THE KITTENS TO THEIR PALS.

At 30 days old, kittens can walk, mew, and play.

Kittens are born with their eyes and ears closed.

# Cheeky puffer fish

Going about its own business, a puffer fish looks very ordinary. This makes it seem like easy prey for many bigger fish. But the puffer fish has a trick up its sleeve. It can quickly fill its body with water and turn into a spiky ball that's almost impossible to eat.

Even if a predator manages to swallow a puffer fish, it could be in for a nasty surprise as some are very poisonous.

**DRAW** MORE PUFFER FISH PUFFING UP.

Puffer fish will only puff up if they're threatened!

Some people like to eat puffer fish. A skilled chef prepares the fish so that all the poison is cut away.

**DRAW** MORE CAMELS WITH ONE OR TWO HUMPS.

Bactrian camels
have two humps.

# One hump or two?

Camels live in the desert, and they can go for days without drinking. People once thought it was because they store water in their humps! This isn't true – the humps are actually filled with fat. But the humps do help camels on long treks because the fat inside them provides the camels with lots of energy.

Dromedary camels have one hump.

# High in the Sky!

The sky is full of living creatures. Many birds fly, and some travel long distances from country to country every year. Insects such as butterflies and some beetles fly. In fact, there are billions of insects in the air at any one time. Bats fly. They are the only furry animals that do!

# wolf-cub club

When wolf cubs are born, they join a pack of about six or seven other wolves, made up of their own family and a few others. The leader of the pack is always their dad. The other positions in the pack are worked out through fights. Wolf cubs practise fighting by playing and wrestling with the other cubs.

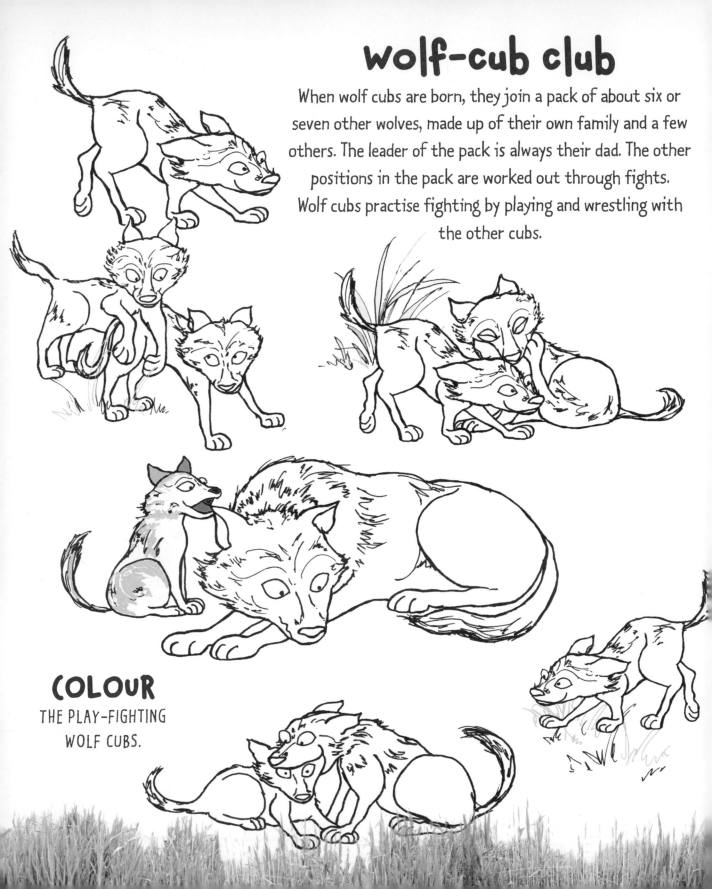

## COLOUR
THE PLAY-FIGHTING
WOLF CUBS.

Wolf cubs stay with their pack for one to three years after they are born.

As wolf cubs grow, they start to eat lumps of meat that have been softened for them by other pack members.

Butterflies drink nectar from flowers through a straw-like tube called a proboscis.

# Beautiful butterflies

If you see a butterfly flying from flower to flower, it's probably looking for nectar to drink. But the butterfly could also be tasting the leaves – with its feet! Once it finds a tasty one, it will lay its eggs there. It does this make sure that its children have something nice to eat as soon as they hatch.

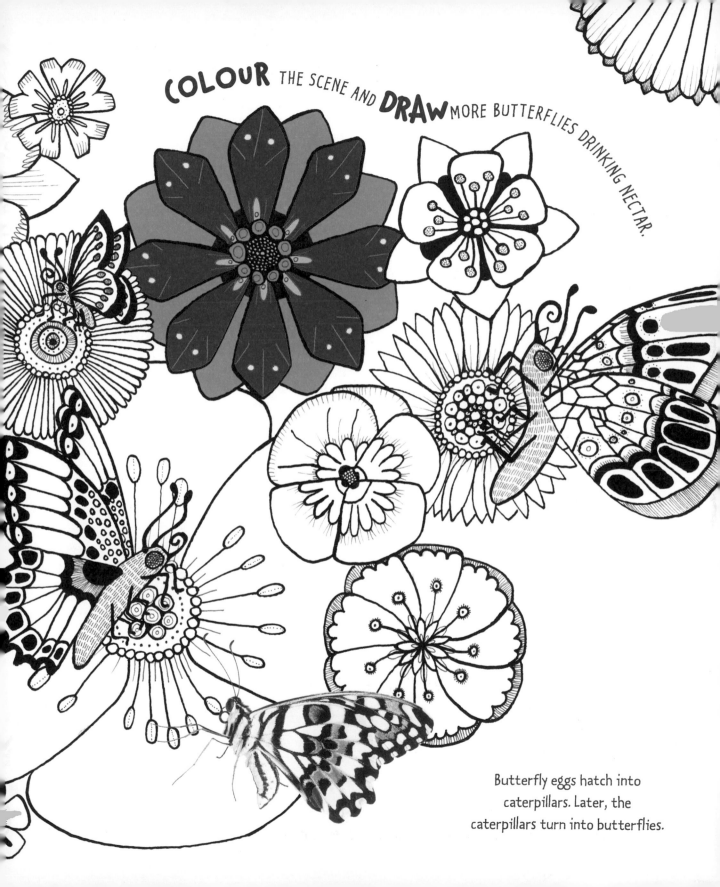

**COLOUR** THE SCENE AND **DRAW** MORE BUTTERFLIES DRINKING NECTAR.

Butterfly eggs hatch into caterpillars. Later, the caterpillars turn into butterflies.

**DRAW** MORE SQUIRRELS GLIDING BETWEEN THE TREES.

In the air, flying squirrels steer themselves by moving their arms, legs, and tail.

# High-flying Squirrels

Is it a bird? Is it a bat? No, it's a flying squirrel! In fact, flying squirrels don't actually fly, but glide. The skin on either side of their body extends from their wrists to their ankles, making a sheet that acts like a parachute. When a squirrel wants to glide down from a tree, it stretches its arms and legs out wide and jumps.

Flying squirrels are expert pilots. They always land safely – even on narrow branches.

# Totally cuckoo

Cunning cuckoos trick other birds into raising their young. They lay their eggs in the nests of other birds. They can colour their egg to match those already in the nest so it is harder for the parent bird to notice it.

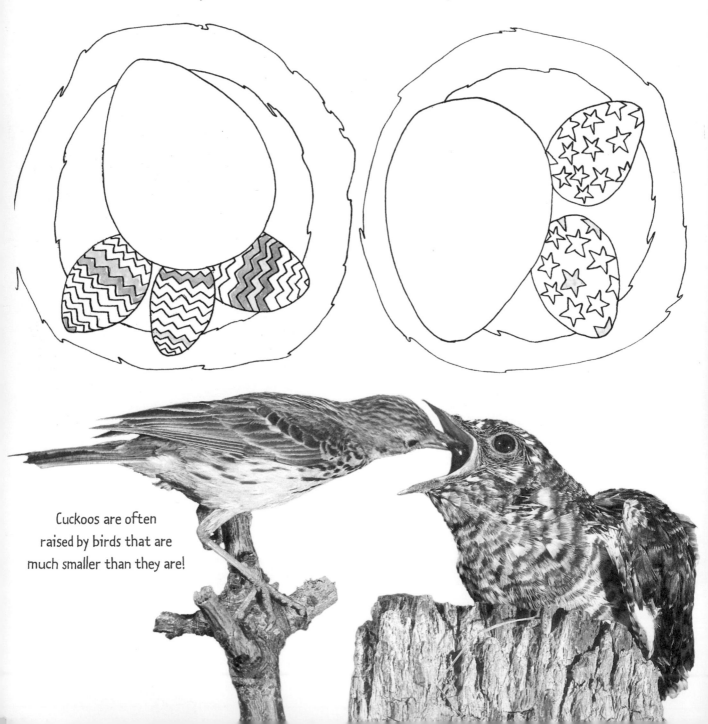

Cuckoos are often raised by birds that are much smaller than they are!

The cuckoo egg is usually much bigger than the eggs already in the nest.

**COLOUR** THE CUCKOO EGG TO MATCH THE EGGS IN THE NEST.

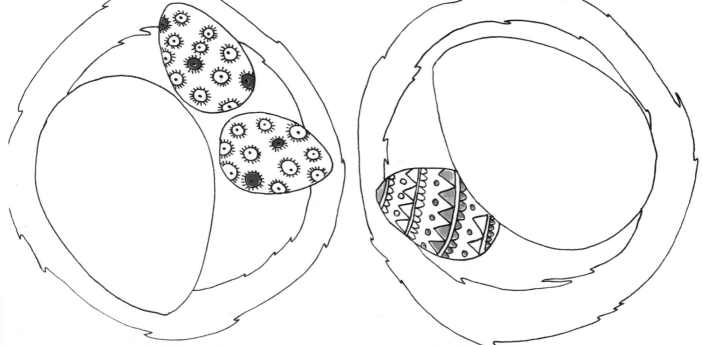

# Mole maze

It's a wonder moles don't get lost in their underground tunnels! Their eyes are small – and it's dark under ground – so they can't see very well at all. They also can't hear very much. But their snout is long and very sensitive so they find their way around using their sense of touch.

Moles spend their time under ground eating, sleeping, and digging.

**HELP** THE MOLES FIND THEIR WAY HOME.

Moles eat worms, insects, and grubs
that they find in the tunnels.

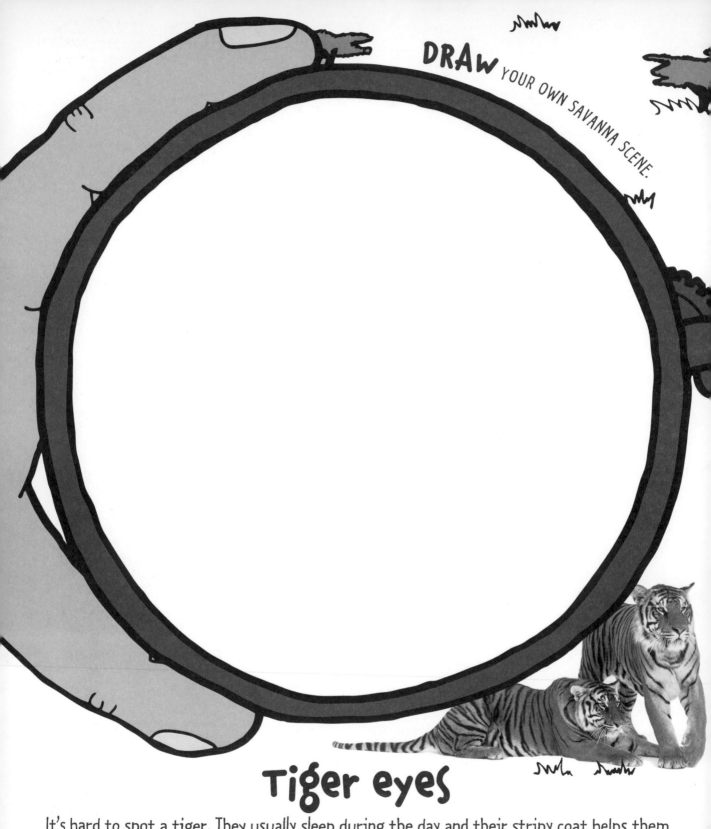

DRAW YOUR OWN SAVANNA SCENE.

# tiger eyes

It's hard to spot a tiger. They usually sleep during the day and their stripy coat helps them hide in woodland and grassy savanna. Their black stripes look like shadows in a sunny landscape.

Tigers are fierce hunters.
They eat small animals like frogs
as well as big ones like antelopes.

Tigers live alone, except for
cubs, who live with their
mother until they are about
one or two years old.

# kangaroo kicks

Kangaroos move around by jumping, using their powerful back legs to travel in big leaps over long distances. Their legs are so strong that the biggest kangaroos can jump up to 12m (39ft) in one bounce. That's farther than the length of two cars!

If a kangaroo could kick a rugby ball, it would probably be the best player on the team!

Kangaroo babies are called joeys. They spend the first months of their life warm and snug in their mother's pouch.

**DRAW** MORE KANGAROOS JUMPING.

**DRAW** MORE BEAVERS IN AND AROUND THEIR LODGE.

Beavers' front teeth never stop growing! They don't get too long though because they are worn down by the wood and bark the beavers gnaw on.

Beavers eat tree bark. In the winter, they store it in the lake, using the water as a refrigerator to keep the bark fresh.

# Beaver builders

Beavers are busy builders. They cut down trees with their strong teeth. Then they use the wood to build dams to create a pool of water. They build their lodge (home) in the pool or on its bank. The lodge has a floor above the water, and it is very warm and snug. The beavers can get to it from the land as well as from the water.

# Busy bees

Bees do an important job – they spread pollen from flower to flower while collecting nectar to take back to their hives. There worker bees turn the nectar into honey. The beehive is a perfect honey store. It's packed with layers of honeycomb made up of thousands of six-sided cells (boxes) for the bees to fill.

**ADD** MORE SIX-SIDED CELLS TO THE HONEYCOMB.

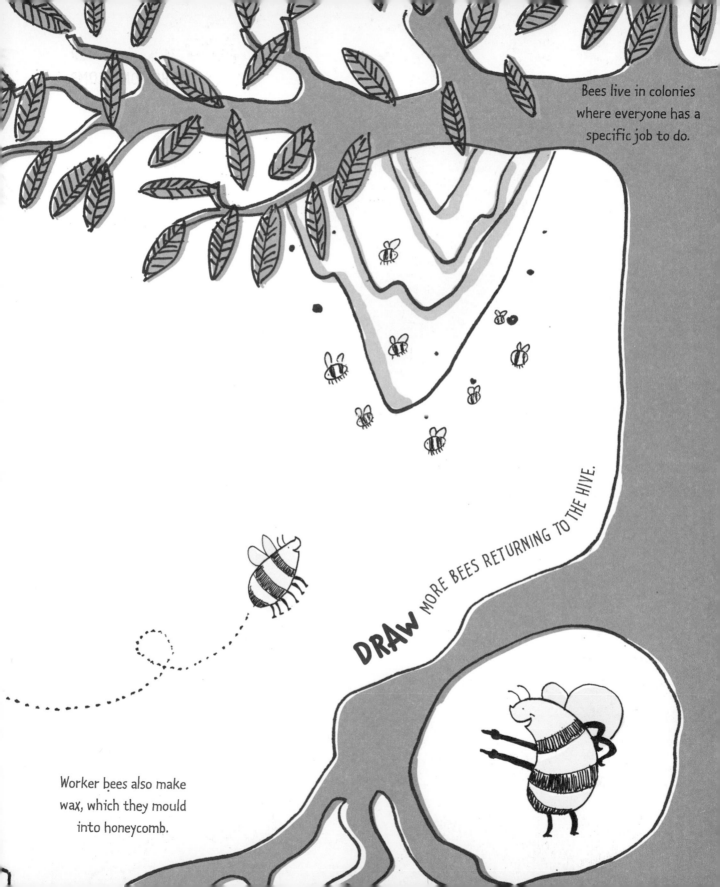

Bees live in colonies where everyone has a specific job to do.

DRAW MORE BEES RETURNING TO THE HIVE.

Worker bees also make wax, which they mould into honeycomb.

Gorillas live in family groups of around 10–15 adults and young.

**CONNECT** THE YOUNG GORILLAS TO THE ADULTS.

# Gorilla campsite

Gorillas spend their days travelling through the rainforest. Every night they build new nests to sleep in. Young gorillas and lighter females sleep in trees while heavier gorillas sleep on the ground.

Gorillas may look scary, but they are actually peaceful plant-eaters.

# Under the Sea!

The world's oceans are huge! From giant whales to tiny creatures, millions of animals call the sea their home. The oceans are so big and deep that no one knows exactly how many sea creatures there are. There could be hundreds of animals that haven't yet been discovered hiding in the depths!

## COLOUR
IN ALL THE SEA CREATURES.

# Crocodile care

Crocodiles are fierce hunters that catch prey in their powerful jaws. You might be surprised to learn that crocodile mums carry their new babies there too! But when they do, they're very gentle and never close their mouth. The babies are very safe between those sharp teeth.

Crocodile babies hatch out of their eggs on land, but mum soon carries them to the water.

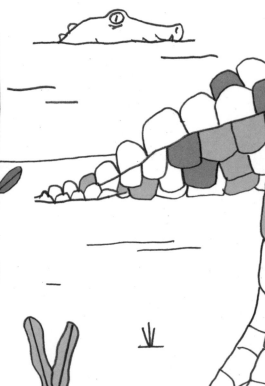

Young crocodiles stay with their mother until they are a few weeks old.

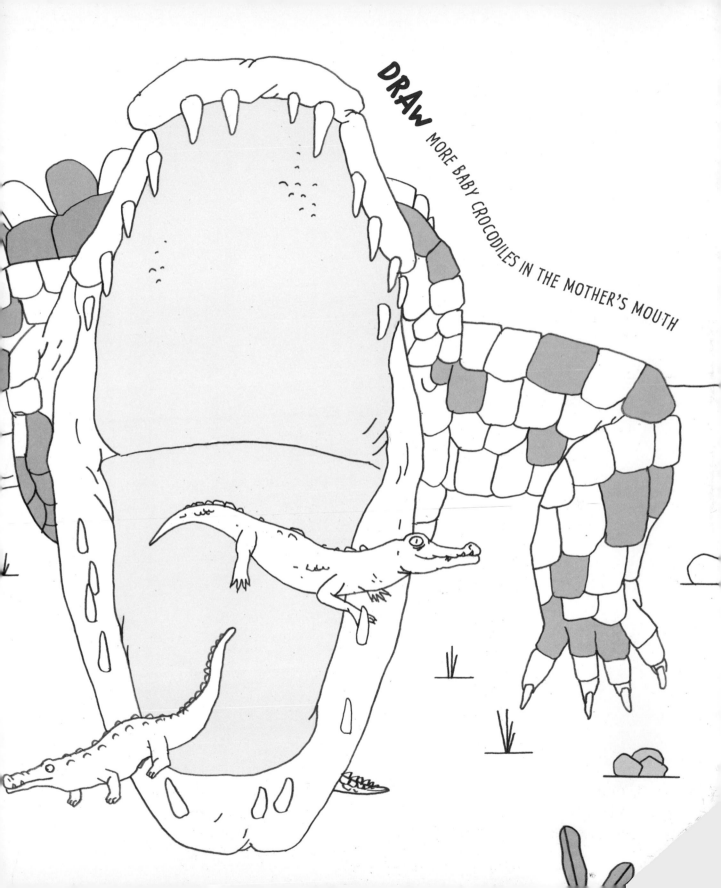

**DRAW** MORE BABY CROCODILES IN THE MOTHER'S MOUTH

# Leap frog!

Ribbit! Frogs are excellent jumpers. They use their powerful back legs to push off, and can jump as far as 40 times their own length. That would be like an adult jumping the length of 6 buses!

Frogs can change direction quickly between hops. This keeps their enemies on their toes!

# DRAW MORE FROGS LEAPING BETWEEN THE LILYPADS.

Frogs are amphibians. This means that they can live both on land and in water.

# Ear Signals

Horses can't tell you how they're feeling. But they can show you, if you just look at their ears. When horses are happy and alert, their ears stand straight up. When they're relaxed, their ears are floppy. And when they're feeling angry or grumpy, their ears lie straight back in warning. That's when it's best to steer clear!

ALERT

ANGRY

DRAW

E HORSES
E STABLES.

Horses are very social animals, and like to live in groups.

**DRAW** MORE HORSES IN THE FIELD.

# Ladybird, ladybird

You might be surprised to learn that ladybirds aren't just red with black spots. They can be many different bright colours, such as orange or yellow. But their bright colouring doesn't just make them look pretty. It also tells birds that they taste horrible. That's why very few birds eat ladybirds.

Ladybirds eat many other insects. This makes them very useful to people, especially on a farm.

DRAW MORE LADYBIRDS AND COLOUR THEM IN.

Ladybirds sleep through the winter, sometimes snoozing in large groups inside tree trunks or outbuildings.

# Lazy hippo days

Hippos like to spend their days keeping cool in the water. Their eyes, ears, and nose are all on the top of their head, so they can stay almost completely under water, and still be able to see, hear, and breathe.

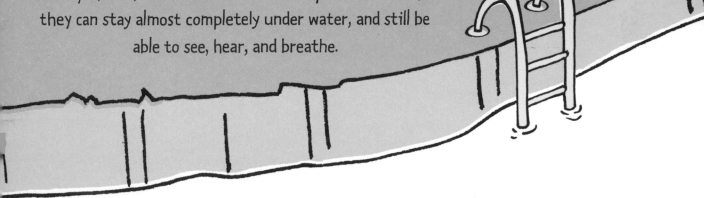

Hippos can close their nostrils and ears when they dive.

Hippos would rather walk along the bottom of a river than swim – unless you give them a rubber ring!

I might have sharp teeth and a huge mouth, but I only eat grass!

**DRAW** MORE HIPPOS STAYING COOL IN THE WATER.

# Pigs in mud

Mmm, there's nothing like a mud bath on a hot day! Pigs splash around in muddy water to keep cool, but mud does another job, too. It sticks to their skin and protects the pigs from the sun's hot rays – a bit like the sunscreen you put on to go the beach!

**DRAW** MORE PIGS
ROLLING AROUND IN THE MUD.

Being covered in mud also stops the pigs from being bitten by insects. All the more reason to jump right in!

Z Z Z
Z
Z

hi my mittens
are dong

# Social Sea otters

Sea otters are social creatures. To stay close to their family and friends, they form floating groups called rafts. Before they go to sleep, sea otters may wrap themselves in a seaweed called kelp. The kelp is attached to the sea floor and keeps the otters from drifting away. Sometimes they even hold each others' paws!

Sea otters float on their back in shallow seas, and they even sleep like this.

**DRAW** MORE SEA OTTERS FORMING RAFTS.

Sea otters spend most of their life in the water. Their thick fur helps them to stay warm.

In the summer, when the ice melts, polar bears eat whatever they can find. This could be land animals, birds, eggs, and plants – or even rubbish left behind by humans!

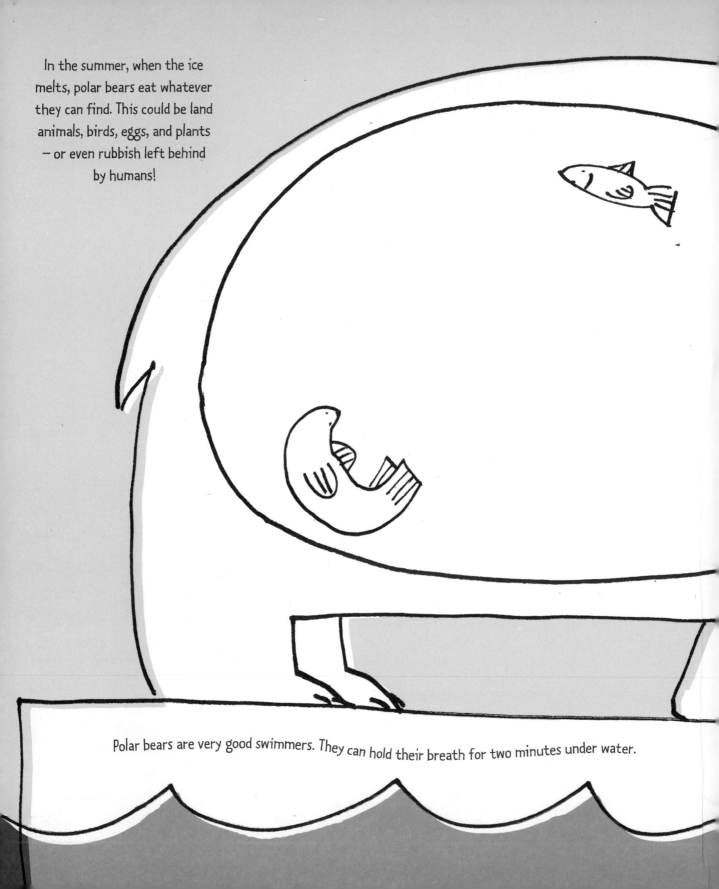

Polar bears are very good swimmers. They can hold their breath for two minutes under water.

DRAW SOME MORE THINGS THAT THIS POLAR BEAR MAY HAVE EATEN FOR HIS DINNER.

# Polar-bear hunt

A polar bear may look cuddly, but it is actually a fierce hunter. It hunts seals that also live on the ice. The polar bear's white coat helps it stay hidden when it follows a seal. If the seal turns around, the polar bear stands very still, and the seal can't see it against the white snow. When the polar bear gets close enough, it quickly snaps up its dinner.

Water spiders eat insects that live in the water. In turn, they might get eaten by frogs or fish.

Water spiders live in slow-moving water where their homes won't be washed away.

**DRAW** MORE WATER SPIDERS – EACH IN THEIR DIVING BELL.

# underwater Spider

Can a spider live under water? The water spider can! It has figured out a clever way of building a home it can breathe in. It spins a web under water and fills it with bubbles of air from the surface that it traps in the hairs on its body. The small bubbles all join up to make a bigger bubble called a diving bell. (Another name for the spider is diving-bell spider.)

The spider lives inside the air-filled diving bell, leaving it only to catch insects and bring down more air bubbles.

When cygnets are small, they're covered in fuzzy grey feathers called down. They don't get their white feathers until they're a bit older.

# Swan love

Swans are true romantics. When they meet the swan of their dreams, they stay together for years, and sometimes even for life. Together they make a nest that's more than 1m (3ft) wide. Up to eight fuzzy swan babies (called cygnets) hatch to swan couples each spring. The babies stay with their parents until they are around six months old.

**DRAW** MORE SWANS WITH THEIR CYGNETS.

Cygnets start swimming soon after they hatch. If they get tired, they may sometimes hitch a ride on mum or dad's back!

# whale watch

Whales are some of the biggest animals on the planet. It might surprise you to learn that some whales don't eat big animals, but huge amounts of tiny shrimps called krill. These whales don't have teeth – they filter their food through big hairy plates (called baleen plates) that hang from the roof of their mouth. These act like a sieve, letting only small bits of food through.

COLOUR
IN ALL THE BIG
AND SMALL
WHALES.

The blue whale is the biggest animal in the world. It is longer than two buses, and its heart can be the size of a car!

**DRAW** SOMETHING
**FANTASTIC**
TO FINISH THE SECTION.

# ACKNOWLEDGMENTS

**Edited by** Alexander Cox, Lorrie Mack, James Mitchem, Laura Palosuo, Lee Wilson, Elizabeth Yeates

**Designed by** Jess Bentall, Charlotte Bull, Jane Ewart, Anna Formanek, Ria Holland, Charlotte Johnson, Sadie Thomas

**Text by** Alexander Cox, Elinor Graham, Wendy Horobin, Susan Maylan, James Mitchem, Ben Morgan, Laura Palosuo, Lee Wilson, Elizabeth Yeates

**Fact checker** Kim Bryan, Wendy Horobin, Darren Naish

**Illustrators** Emma Atkinson, Carolyn Bayley, Evannave, Holly Blackman, Amber Cassidy, Helen Dodsworth, Carly Epworth, Nic Farrell, Sean Gee, Rob Griffiths, Chris Howker, Barney Ibbotson, Jake McDonald, Peter Todd, Dan Woodger, Jay Wright

## PICTURE CREDITS

The publisher would like to thank the following for their kind permission to reproduce their photographs:

(Key: a-above; b-below/bottom; c-center; f-far; l-left; r-right; t-top)

**Dorling Kindersley**: Jamie Marshall 15r; NASA / JPL 16bl; International Robotics 7ca, 7cra, 101bl; Lindsey Stock 20cl; Young 42clb; Milo and Snoop 51tl; NASA 56bc; Judith Miller / Freeman's 59tr; Oxford University Museum of Natural History 59tl; Bethany Dawn 62–63; Stephen Oliver 63ftl; Natural History Museum, London 73cr; Jamie Marshall 78–79; Royal Armouries 85bl; Josef Hlasek 99bl; Whipsnade Zoo, Bedfordshire 99cr; Rough Guides 106c, 106l.

All other images © Dorling Kindersley

For further information see: **www.dkimages.com**

GOODBYE!